Math Expressions

Volume 2

Developed by
The Children's Math Worlds Research Project

PROJECT DIRECTOR AND AUTHOR
Dr. Karen C. Fuson

This material is based upon work supported by the
National Science Foundation
under Grant Numbers
ESI-9816320, REC-9806020, and RED-935373.

Any opinions, findings, and conclusions, or recommendations expressed in this material
are those of the author and do not necessarily reflect the views of the National Science Foundation.

HOUGHTON MIFFLIN HARCOURT

Teacher Reviewers

Kindergarten
Patricia Stroh Sugiyama
Wilmette, Illinois

Barbara Wahle
Evanston, Illinois

Grade 1
Sandra Budson
Newton, Massachusetts

Janet Pecci
Chicago, Illinois

Megan Rees
Chicago, Illinois

Grade 2
Molly Dunn
Danvers, Massachusetts

Agnes Lesnick
Hillside, Illinois

Rita Soto
Chicago, Illinois

Grade 3
Jane Curran
Honesdale, Pennsylvania

Sandra Tucker
Chicago, Illinois

Grade 4
Sara Stoneberg Llibre
Chicago, Illinois

Sheri Roedel
Chicago, Illinois

Grade 5
Todd Atler
Chicago, Illinois

Leah Barry
Norfolk, Massachusetts

Special Thanks

Special thanks to the many teachers, students, parents, principals, writers, researchers, and work-study students who participated in the Children's Math Worlds Research Project over the years.

Credits

(t) © Charles Cormany/Workbook Stock/Jupiter Images, (b) Noah Strycker/Shutterstock

llustrative art: Robin Boyer/Deborah Wolfe, LTD; Dave Clegg, Spatial Graphics, Tim Johnson
Technical art: Nesbitt Graphics, Inc.
Photos: Nesbitt Graphics, Inc.; Page 309 © Anna Clopet/Corbis

VOLUME 2 CONTENTS

Continued ▶

* This lesson consists only of activities from the Teacher Edition.

Mini Unit 12 Metric Measurement and 3-D Shapes

Unit 13 Multiplication and Fractions

Groups and Arrays

Symmetry and Fractions

The Nature of Chance

Continued ▶

* This lesson consists only of activities from the Teacher Edition.

8-1

Name

Class Activity

► Name Quadrilaterals

Vocabulary

rectangle quadrilateral

	Is it a **square**? Explain.	Is it a **rectangle**? Explain.	Is it a **parallelogram**? Explain.	Is it a **quadrilateral**? Explain.
1.	Yes. It has 4 equal sides and the corners are square.	colk	novn	
2.				
3.				
4.				

UNIT 8 LESSON 1

Diagonals of Quadrilaterals **257**

Class Activity

Name Lauren F#19

Vocabulary

diagonal

▶ **Draw Diagonals**

> A line segment that connects opposite corners of a quadrilateral is called a **diagonal**.

5. Draw a diagonal in this square.

6. What shapes are formed by drawing a diagonal in a square?

_____

7. What are your observations about the two shapes that are formed?

_____

_____

8. Draw a diagonal in this rectangle.

9. What shapes are formed by drawing a diagonal in a rectangle?

_____

Diagonals of Quadrilaterals

Dear Family,

Your child is working on a geometry unit about dividing quadrilaterals into smaller shapes by drawing diagonals and line segments that connect the midpoints of opposite sides. The main goal of this unit is to help children develop their spatial abilities.

Diagonals are line segments that join opposite corners of a quadrilateral.

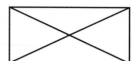

A midpoint divides a line segment into two equal parts.

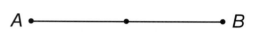

When you join the midpoints of opposite sides, you divide a quadrilateral into four parts.

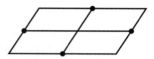

Encourage your child to look for quadrilaterals in your home and neighborhood. Ask your child to predict what shapes will be formed by drawing diagonals in the quadrilaterals or by connecting the midpoints of opposite sides.

For example, ask your child to describe the shape of a sandwich before you cut it. Ask your child to then predict what shapes will be formed if you cut the sandwich along the diagonals or along the line segments made by joining the midpoints on opposite sides.

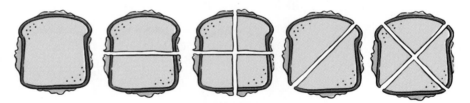

In this unit, your child will be asked to draw diagonals on three identical shapes. Your child will draw a different diagonal in each of the first two shapes and draw both diagonals in the third shape.

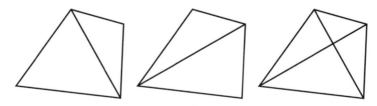

If you have any questions or comments, please call or write to me.

Sincerely,
Your child's teacher

Estimada familia:

Su niño está trabajando en una unidad de geometría. Aprenderá a dividir cuadriláteros en figuras más pequeñas dibujando diagonales y segmentos que unen los puntos medios de lados opuestos. El objetivo principal de esta unidad es ayudar a los niños a desarrollar su sentido espacial.

Las diagonales son segmentos que unen vértices opuestos de un cuadrilátero.

Los puntos medios dividen un segmento en dos partes iguales.

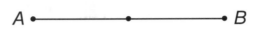

$A \bullet \longrightarrow \bullet B$

Cuando se unen los puntos medios de lados opuestos se divide el cuadrilátero en cuatro partes.

Anime a su niño a buscar cuadriláteros en la casa y en el vecindario. Pídale que prediga qué figuras se formarán al dibujar diagonales en los cuadriláteros o al unir los puntos medios de lados opuestos.

Por ejemplo, pida a su niño que describa la figura de un sándwich antes de cortarlo. Pídale que prediga qué figuras se formarán is corta el sándwich por las diagonales o por los segmentos formados al unir los puntos medios con los lados opuestos.

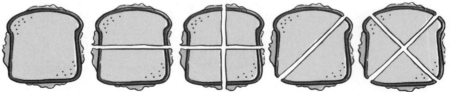

En esta unidad su niño deberá dibujar diagonales en tres figuras idénticas. Se le pedirá que dibuje una diagonal diferente en cada una de las primeras dos figuras y que dibuje ambas diagonales en la tercera figura.

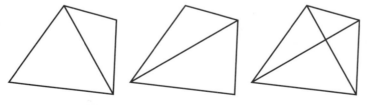

Si tiene alguna pregunta o comentario, por favor comuníquese conmigo.

Atentamente,
El maestro de su niño

Diagonals of Quadrilaterals

Class Activity

▶ **Explore Methods of Finding Midpoints**

The **midpoint** of a line segment divides the line segment into two equal parts.

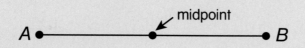

Use at least two different ways to find the midpoint of each line segment and draw a dot at that point.

1. *J* •————————————• *K*

2. *C* •————————• *D*

3. *E* •————————————————————• *F*

4. *P* •————————————————————————————• *Q*

5. **Explain Your Thinking** Describe two of the ways you used to find the midpoints of the line segments above.

_____

_____

_____

_____

_____

▶ **Connect Midpoints**

6. Mark the midpoints of two **opposite sides**.

7. What shapes do you think you will see when you connect the midpoints?

    _____

8. Connect the midpoints. Describe the shapes you see.

    _____

9. Mark the midpoints of the other two opposite sides.

10. Connect the midpoints. What shapes do you see?

    _____

11. How are these shapes like the shapes in the first square? How are they different?

    _____

    _____

Connect Midpoints in Quadrilaterals

Class Activity

► Add Line Segments to Shapes

Draw one diagonal.	Draw the other diagonal.	Draw both diagonals.
1.		
2.		
3.		
4.		

Name _____

Class Activity

▶ Add Line Segments to Shapes

Use estimation to find the midpoints.

	Connect the midpoints of two opposite sides.	Connect the midpoints of the other two sides.	Draw both line segments.
5.			
6.			
7.			
8.			

Practice with Diagonals and Connecting Midpoints

Draw one diagonal.	Draw the other diagonal.	Draw both diagonals.
1.		
2.		

3. Find the midpoint of the line segment and draw a dot at that point.

H •————————————————————————————• I

4. Draw one diagonal in the square.

Describe the new shapes.

_____

_____

5. Draw two diagonals in the parallelogram.

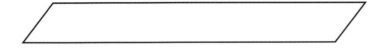

Describe the new shapes.

_____

_____

6. Draw two diagonals in this quadrilateral.

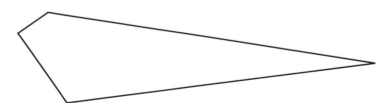

Describe the new shapes.

_____

_____

7. Connect the midpoints of two opposite sides.

Describe the new shapes.

_____

_____

8. Connect the midpoints of two opposite sides. Then connect the midpoints of the other two sides.

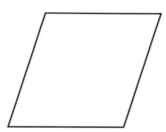

Describe the new shapes.

_____

_____

9. Connect the midpoints of two opposite sides. Then connect the midpoints of the other two sides.

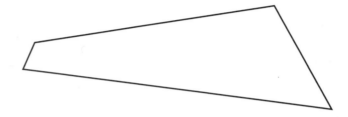

Describe the new shapes.

_____

_____

10. **Extended Response** Use two different methods to find the midpoint of this line segment.

S •————————————————————• T

Describe both methods.

_____

_____

_____

_____

_____

_____

_____

_____

Test

Dive the Deep

$11 - 6 = \boxed{5}$ $12 - \boxed{6} = 6$ $13 - 8 = \boxed{5}$

$12 - 7 = \boxed{5}$ $17 - \boxed{8} = 9$ $15 - 6 = \boxed{9}$

$12 - 9 = \boxed{3}$ $13 - \boxed{5} = 8$ $11 - 9 = \boxed{2}$

$13 - 4 = \boxed{9}$ $14 - \boxed{6} = 8$ $13 - 9 = \boxed{4}$

$11 - 5 = \boxed{6}$ $17 - \boxed{9} = 8$ $15 - 7 = \boxed{8}$

$14 - 9 = \boxed{5}$ $11 - \boxed{8} = 3$ $14 - 8 = \boxed{6}$

$14 - 7 = \boxed{7}$ $12 - \boxed{4} = 8$ $12 - 5 = \boxed{7}$

$16 - 7 = \boxed{9}$ $16 - \boxed{8} = 8$ $11 - 3 = \boxed{8}$

$11 - 7 = \boxed{4}$ $15 - \boxed{7} = 8$ $13 - 6 = \boxed{7}$

$12 - 3 = \boxed{9}$ $16 - \boxed{9} = 7$ $18 - 9 = \boxed{9}$

$13 - 7 = \boxed{6}$ $11 - \boxed{4} = 7$ $12 - 8 = \boxed{4}$

Dive the Deep

$11 - 5 = \boxed{6}$

$12 - \boxed{6} = 6$

$13 - 5 = \boxed{8}$

$12 - 5 = \boxed{7}$

$17 - \boxed{9} = 8$

$15 - 9 = \boxed{6}$

$12 - 3 = \boxed{9}$

$13 - \boxed{8} = 5$

$11 - 2 = \boxed{9}$

$13 - 9 = \boxed{4}$

$14 - \boxed{8} = 6$

$13 - 4 = \boxed{9}$

$11 - 6 = \boxed{5}$

$17 - \boxed{8} = 9$

$15 - 8 = \boxed{7}$

$14 - 5 = \boxed{9}$

$11 - \boxed{3} = 8$

$14 - 6 = \boxed{8}$

$14 - 7 = \boxed{7}$

$12 - \boxed{8} = 4$

$12 - 7 = \boxed{5}$

$16 - 9 = \boxed{7}$

$16 - \boxed{8} = 8$

$11 - 8 = \boxed{3}$

$11 - 4 = \boxed{7}$

$15 - \boxed{8} = 7$

$13 - 7 = \boxed{6}$

$12 - 9 = \boxed{3}$

$16 - \boxed{7} = 9$

$18 - 9 = \boxed{9}$

$13 - 6 = \boxed{7}$

$11 - \boxed{7} = 4$

$12 - 4 = \boxed{8}$

Dive the Deep

Class Activity

► Explain the Expanded Method

Mr. Green likes this method. Explain what he does.

Step 1	Step 2	Step 3

Step 1
$$64 = 60 + 4$$
$$-28 = 20 + 8$$

|||||| | ∘∘∘∘

Step 2
$$64 = \cancel{6}\overset{50}{0} + \overset{14}{\cancel{4}}$$
$$-28 = 20 + 8$$

|||||| ⚹   ∘∘∘∘

Step 3
$$64 = \cancel{6}\overset{50}{0} + \overset{14}{\cancel{4}}$$
$$-28 = 20 + 8$$
$$30 + 6 = 36$$

卌||| ⚹   ∘∘∘∘

► Try the Expanded Method

Show your work numerically and with a Proof Drawing.

1. $$\begin{array}{r} 42 \\ -19 \\ \hline \end{array}$$

2. $$\begin{array}{r} 75 \\ -46 \\ \hline \end{array}$$

3. $$\begin{array}{r} 81 \\ -37 \\ \hline \end{array}$$

Class Activity

Name _____

▶ Explain the Ungroup First Method

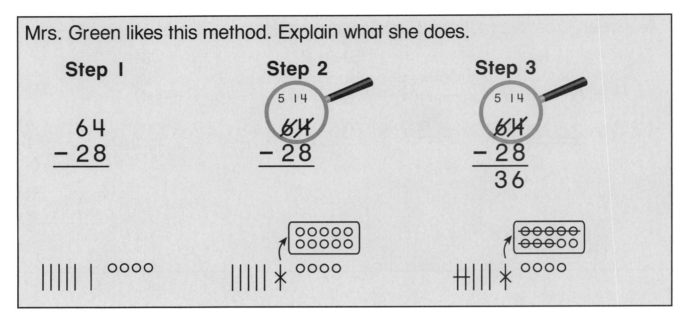

Mrs. Green likes this method. Explain what she does.

Step 1	Step 2	Step 3

▶ Try the Ungroup First Method

Show your work numerically and with a Proof Drawing.

4. $\begin{array}{r} 42 \\ -19 \\ \hline \end{array}$

5. $\begin{array}{r} 75 \\ -46 \\ \hline \end{array}$

6. $\begin{array}{r} 81 \\ -37 \\ \hline \end{array}$

Two Methods of Subtraction

Dear Family,

Your child is now learning how to subtract 2-digit numbers. The big mystery is how to get enough ones in order to subtract. As with addition, children first use methods they invent themselves. We have found that children take pride in using their own methods.

In this program, children learn two methods for 2-digit subtraction, but children may use any method that they understand, can explain, and can do fairly quickly.

Expanded Method	Ungroup First Method
Step 1 "Expand" each number to show that it is made up of tens and ones. $$64 = 60 + 4$$ $$-28 = 20 + 8$$	**Step 1** Check to see if there are enough ones to subtract from. If not, ungroup by opening up 1 of the 6 tens in 64 to be 10 ones. 4 ones plus these new 10 ones make 14 ones. We draw a "magnifying glass" around the top number to focus children on whether they need to ungroup before subtraction.
Step 2 Check to see if there are enough ones to subtract from. If not, ungroup a ten into 10 ones and add it to the existing ones. $$\overset{50 \;+\; 14}{64 = \cancel{60} + \cancel{4}}$$ $$-28 = 20 + 8$$	
Step 3 Subtract to find the answer. Children may subtract from left to right or right to left. $$\overset{50 \;+\; 14}{64 = \cancel{60} + \cancel{4}}$$ $$-28 = 20 + 8$$ $$30 + 6 = 36$$	**Step 2** Subtract to find the answer. Children may subtract from left to right or right to left. 

In explaining any method they use, children are expected to use "tens and ones" language. This shows that they understand they are subtracting 2 tens from 5 tens (not 2 from 5) and 8 ones from 14 ones.

Please call if you have any questions or comments.

Sincerely,
Your child's teacher

Carta a la familia

Estimada familia:

Su niño está aprendiendo a restar números de 2 dígitos. El misterio es cómo obtener suficientes unidades para poder restar. como en la suma, los niños primero usan métodos que ellos mismos inventan. Hemos notado que los niños se sienten orgullosos de usar sus propios métodos.

En este programa, los niños aprenden dos métodos para la resta con números de 2 dígitos, pero pueden usar cualquier método que comprendan, puedan explicar y puedan hacer relativamente rápido.

Método extendido	Método de desagrupar primero
Paso 1 "Extender" cada número para mostrar que consta de decenas y unidades. $$64 = 60 + 4$$ $$-28 = 20 + 8$$ **Paso 2** Observar si hay suficientes unidades para restar. Si no las hay, desagrupar una decena para formar 10 unidades y sumarla a las unidades existentes. $$\begin{array}{c} 50 \ + \ 14 \\ 64 = \cancel{60} + \cancel{4} \\ -28 = 20 + 8 \end{array}$$ **Paso 3** Restar para hallar la respuesta. Los niños pueden restar de izquierda a derecha o de derecha a izquierda. $$\begin{array}{c} 50 \ + \ 14 \\ 64 = \cancel{60} + \cancel{4} \\ -28 = 20 + 8 \\ \hline 30 + 6 = 36 \end{array}$$	**Paso 1** Observar si hay suficientes unidades para restar. Si no las hay, entonces desagrupar duna de las 6 decenas en 64 para obtener 10 unidades. 4 unidades más las 10 unidades nuevas hacen 14 unidades. Dibujamos una "lupa" alrededor del número superior para que los niños piensen si necesitan desagrupar antes de restar.  **Paso 2** Restar para hallar la respuesta. Los niños pueden restar de izquierda a derecha o de derecha a izquierda. 

Cuando los niños explican el método que usan, deben usar un lenguaje relacionado con "decenas y unidades". Esto demuestra que comprenden que están restando 2 decenas de 5 decenas (no 2 de 5) y 8 unidades de 14 unidades.

Si tiene alguna duda o comentario, por favor comuníquese conmigo.

Atentamente,
El maestro de su niño

Two Methods of Subtraction

Class Activity

Name _____

► **Addition and Subtraction Story Problems**

Draw a Math Mountain to solve each story problem. Show how you add or subtract.

Show your work.

___

1. Teresa had 85 blocks. Then she found 47 more under the couch. How many blocks does Teresa have now?

   [___] _____

   label

___

2. Krina's class made 163 masks. They hung 96 of them in the library. How many masks do they have left?

   [___] _____

   label

___

3. Andy's plant was 138 inches tall. It grew 27 inches. How many inches tall is his plant now?

   [___] _____

   label

___

4. The school store had 144 glue sticks. They sold 79 so far this year. How many glue sticks do they have left?

   [___] _____

   label

Going Further

Name _____

▶ Estimate to Find the Answer

Use any method to **estimate** the solutions to
exercises 1–4. Write the estimate on the line.
Then use the estimate to help you match the
exercise to its answer.

1. _____

$$\begin{array}{r} 92 \\ -\ 17 \end{array}$$ •   • 9

2. _____

$$\begin{array}{r} 72 \\ +\ 52 \end{array}$$ •   • 93

3. _____

$$\begin{array}{r} 33 \\ 22 \\ +\ 38 \end{array}$$ •   • 124

4. _____

$$\begin{array}{r} 48 \\ -\ 39 \end{array}$$ •   • 75

Jason has 38 cartoon videos and 19 movie videos.
He wants to buy a cabinet that will hold 70 videos.

5. About how many videos does he have in all? _____

6. Will they all fit in the cabinet? _____

Story Problems with Addition and Subtraction

Class Activity

▶ **Find Equations for Math Mountains**

1. Write all of the equations for 83, 59, and 24.

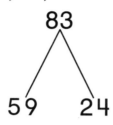

$$59 + 24 = 83$$

$$83 = 59 + 24$$

2. Write all of the equations for 142, 96, and 46.

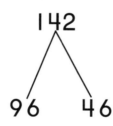

$$96 + 46 = 142$$

$$142 = 96 + 46$$

3. **On the Back** Show how you can subtract to find the unknown partner for 96 + ☐ = 142.

Math Mountain Equations with Larger Numbers

Class Activity

▶ Practice the Adding Up Method

Solve each story problem.

Show your work.

---

1. Justin read 162 comics. Trina read
   93 comics. How many more comics
   did Justin read than Trina?

   ☐ _____
   label

---

2. Maya made 64 drawings. Philip
   made 132 drawings. How many
   fewer drawings did Maya make
   than Philip?

   ☐ _____
   label

---

3. There were 187 birds in the zoo.
   The zoo received some more birds,
   and now they have 246 birds. How
   many birds did the zoo receive?

   ☐ _____
   label

---

4. Rita had 121 pens. She gave some
   pens to her friends. Now she has
   75 pens. How many pens did Rita
   give away?

   ☐ _____
   label

Extra Practice

Name _____

▶ **Alphabet Math Puzzle**

Add or subtract. Then, solve the alphabet puzzle by using the answer for the exercise to find the next letter in the puzzle.

A = $\begin{array}{r} 42 \\ +\ 79 \\ \hline \end{array}$

O = $\begin{array}{r} 142 \\ -\ 17 \\ \hline \end{array}$

H = $\begin{array}{r} 137 \\ -\ 76 \\ \hline \end{array}$

M = $\begin{array}{r} 125 \\ +\ 38 \\ \hline \end{array}$

C = $\begin{array}{r} 126 \\ -\ 84 \\ \hline \end{array}$

N = $\begin{array}{r} 121 \\ -\ 37 \\ \hline \end{array}$

D = $\begin{array}{r} 84 \\ +\ 58 \\ \hline \end{array}$

A = $\begin{array}{r} 163 \\ -\ 75 \\ \hline \end{array}$

T = $\begin{array}{r} 88 \\ +\ 49 \\ \hline \end{array}$

$\underset{\text{}}{\text{I}}$ $\underset{42}{\quad}$ $\underset{121}{\quad}$ $\underset{84}{\quad}$ $\underset{142}{\quad}$ $\underset{125}{\quad}$ $\underset{163}{\quad}$ $\underset{88}{\quad}$ $\underset{137}{\quad}$ $\underset{61}{\quad}$!

More Story Problems with Unknown Partners

Unit Test

Name _____

Count the money.

1.

   25¢   50¢   75¢   85¢   _____   _____   _____   _____   _____

2.

   _____   _____   _____   _____   _____   _____   _____   _____   _____

3.

   _____   _____   _____   _____   _____   _____   _____   _____   _____

Subtract. Ungroup if you need to.

4. 63
  − 27

5. 84
  − 19

6. 92
  − 46

7. 57
  − 25

Name _____

Subtract.

8. $\begin{array}{r} 100 \\ -\ 18 \\ \hline \end{array}$

9. $\begin{array}{r} 200 \\ -\ 43 \\ \hline \end{array}$

10. $\begin{array}{r} 179 \\ -\ 81 \\ \hline \end{array}$

11. $\begin{array}{r} 198 \\ -\ 56 \\ \hline \end{array}$

12. $\begin{array}{r} 130 \\ -\ 67 \\ \hline \end{array}$

13. $\begin{array}{r} 104 \\ -\ 13 \\ \hline \end{array}$

14. $\begin{array}{r} 156 \\ -\ 39 \\ \hline \end{array}$

15. $\begin{array}{r} 143 \\ -\ 84 \\ \hline \end{array}$

Vocabulary
congruent

► **Congruent Figures**

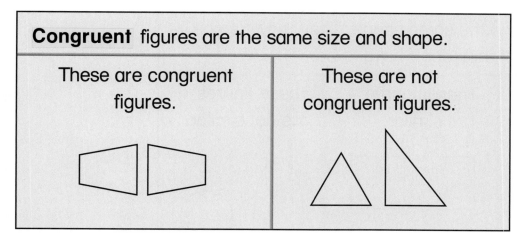

Congruent figures are the same size and shape.

| These are congruent figures. | These are not congruent figures. |

Which two figures are congruent?

1. Figures _____ and _____ are congruent.

2. Figures _____ and _____ are congruent.

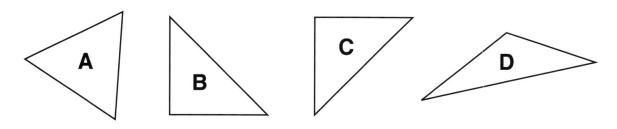

3. Figures _____ and _____ are congruent.

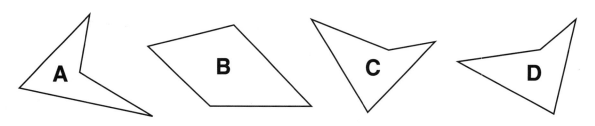

Name _____

Class Activity

Vocabulary
similar

▶ Similar Figures

Similar figures are the same shape. They may also be the same size, but they don't have to be.

These figures are similar.	These figures are similar.	These figures are not similar.
	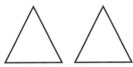	

Are the two figures similar? Write _similar_ or _not similar._

4.

5.

_____   _____

6.
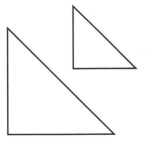

7.
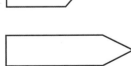

_____   _____

Compare Shapes

Name _____

Class Activity

▶ **Sort Figures**

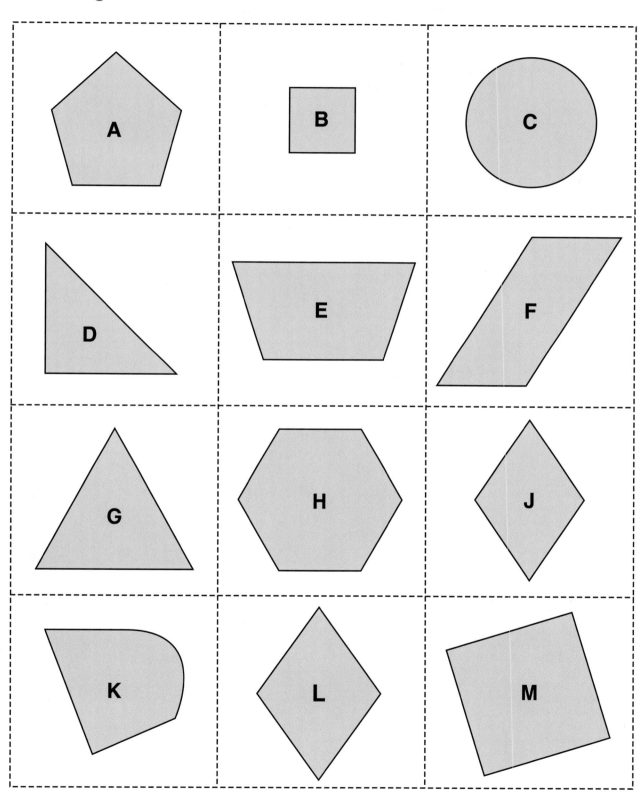

Compare Shapes **317**

Compare Shapes

Dear Family,

Your child is working on a geometry unit about congruent figures: figures that are the same size and shape. The unit also covers similar figures: figures that are the same shape but not necessarily the same size.

Your child will be sliding figures up, down, left, and right; flipping figures over horizontal and vertical lines; and turning figures around a point.

He or she will also explore different types of patterns, including repeating patterns, growing patterns, and motion patterns (slides, flips, and turns).

Your child will be asked to find the area of figures in square centimeters by counting the number of squares on centimeter-grid paper that a figure covers.

You can help reinforce your child's math learning at home.

• Encourage your child to work on jigsaw puzzles to practice sliding, flipping, and turning figures.

• Have your child find the area of tiled floors in square units by counting square tiles.

• Help your child identify patterns in fabrics, nature, music, and art.

• Create patterns using objects like buttons, paper clips, or coins. Ask your child to continue the pattern. Or you can remove one piece from the pattern and ask your child to identify the missing piece.

If you have any questions or comments, please call or write to me.

Sincerely,
Your child's teacher

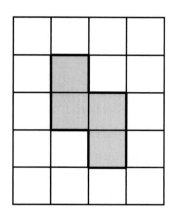

Area of shaded figure =
4 square centimeters

Estimada familia:

Su niño está trabajando en una unidad de geometría sobre figuras congruentes: figuras que tienen el mismo tamaño y forma. La unidad también incluye figuras semejantes: figuras que tienen la misma forma pero no necesariamente el mismo tamaño.

Su niño trasladará figuras hacia arriba, hacia abajo, hacia la izquierda y hacia la derecha; invertirá figuras sobre rectas horizontales y verticales y hará girar figuras alrededor de un punto.

También explorará diferentes tipos de patrones, incluidos patrones que se repiten, patrones que aumentan y patrones de movimiento (traslaciones, inversiones y giros).

Se le pedirá a su niño que halle el área de figuras en centímetros cuadrados contando el número de cuadrados de un papel cuadriculado que están cubiertos por una figura.

Usted puede ayudar a que su niño refuerce el aprendizaje de matemáticas en casa.

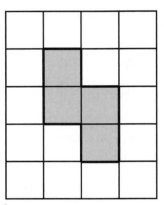

Área de la figura sombreada = 4 centímetros cuadrados

• Anime a su niño a trabajar con rompecabezas para practicar la traslación, la inversión y el giro de figuras.

• Pídale a su niño que halle el área de pisos de baldosas en unidades cuadradas, contando baldosas cuadradas.

• Ayude a su niño a identificar patrones en las telas, la naturaleza, la música y el arte.

• Haga patrones utilizando objetos como botones, sujetapapeles o monedas. Pida a su niño que continúe el patrón. También, puede quitar una pieza del patrón y pedirle al niño que identifique la pieza que falta.

Si tiene alguna pregunta o comentario, por favor comuníquese conmigo.

Atentamente,
El maestro de su niño

Compare Shapes

Vocabulary

slide

▶ **Identify Slides**

You can **slide** a figure right or left along a straight line.

You can slide a figure up or down along a straight line.

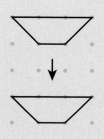

Does each picture show a slide? Write *yes* or *no.*

1.

2.

3.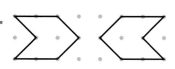

4.

Class Activity

Name _____

Vocabulary
flip
horizontal line
vertical line

► Identify Flips

You can **flip** a figure over a **horizontal line**.

You can flip a figure over a **vertical line**.

Does each picture show a flip over the line? Write *yes* or *no*.

5.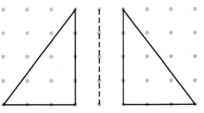

_____

6.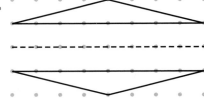

_____

7.

_____

8.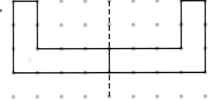

_____

Motion Geometry

Class Activity

Name _____

► **Identify Turns**

You can **turn** or **rotate** a figure around a point.

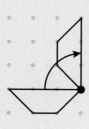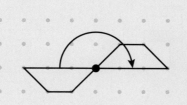

Does each picture show a turn around the point?
Write *yes* or *no*.

9.

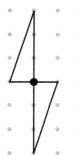

10.

11.

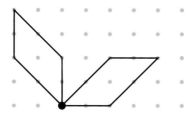

12.

Class Activity

Vocabulary
slide
flip
turn

► **Identify Slides, Flips, and Turns**

You can **slide, flip,** or **turn** a figure to make a pattern.

Write *slide, flip,* or *turn* to describe each pattern.

13.

_____

14.

_____

15.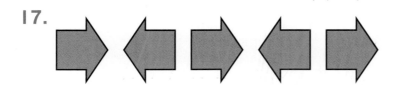

_____

16.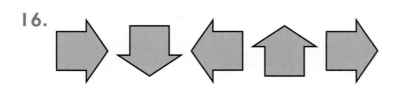

_____

17.

_____

18.

_____

Motion Geometry

► Extend Patterns

Draw the next figure in the pattern.

19.

_____

20.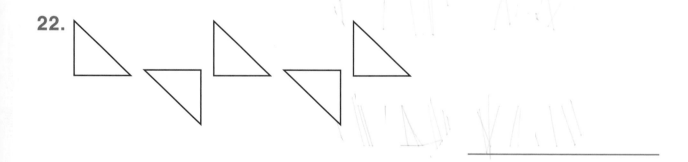

_____

21.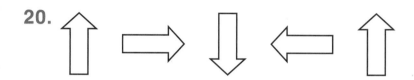

_____

22.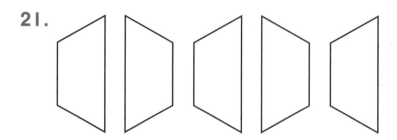

_____

23.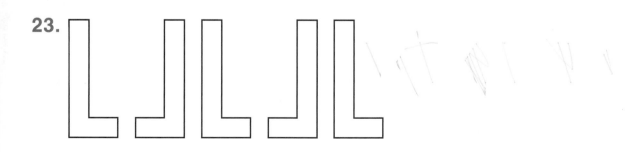

_____

Name _____

Going Further

Vocabulary

tessellation

▶ Explore Tessellations

A **tessellation** is a pattern made by congruent polygons that fit together exactly to cover a surface.

A tessellation is like a tiling pattern that covers a floor.

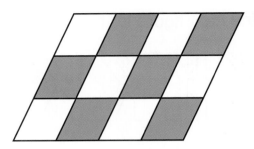

1. Use your ruler to continue the pattern to make a tessellation of triangles.

   Color the triangles to make a pattern.

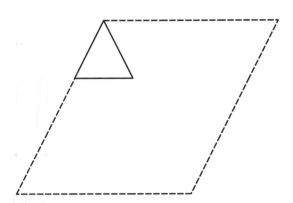

2. Use your ruler to draw more figures to extend this tessellation. Color the tessellation to make a pattern.

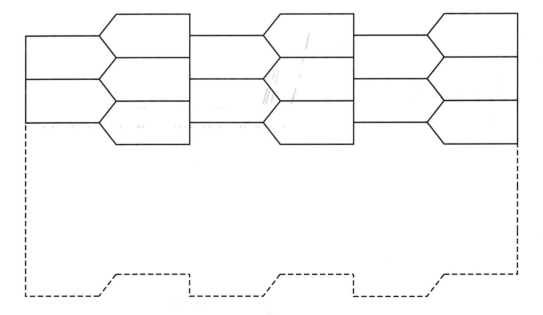

Motion Geometry

Name _____

Class Activity

Say each pattern aloud.
Draw what comes next.

1.

2.

3.

Draw what comes next in each **growing pattern**.

4.

5.

6.

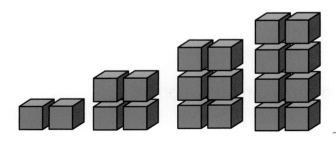

Class Activity

Name

Vocabulary

motion pattern

Draw what comes next in each **motion pattern**.

1. ➡⬇⬅⬆ ➡⬇⬅⬆ ➡⬇⬅⬆ ➡⬇⬅⬆ _____

2.

_____

3. Trace a square by an edge of the grid.

   Move it and trace it 4 times.

4. Draw and cut out a letter. Trace it to show a motion pattern.

Patterns with Shapes

Class Activity

▶ **Count Square Units**

Vocabulary
area
square units

I square unit

Cover each figure with **square units**
and count them to find the **area**.

1.

Area = ☐ square units

2.

Area = ☐ square units

3.

Area = ☐ square units

Name _____

Class Activity

Vocabulary

square centimeter

▶ Count Square Centimeters

You can measure area in **square centimeters**.
A square centimeter is a square with sides that
measure 1 cm.

1 square centimeter

Count the number of squares in each shaded figure to
find the area in square centimeters.

4.

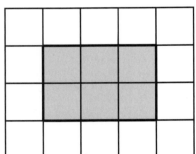

Area = ☐ square centimeters

5.

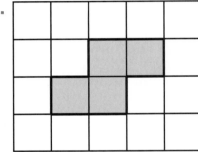

Area = ☐ square centimeters

6.

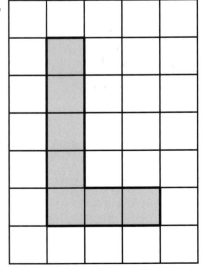

Area = ☐ square centimeters

7.

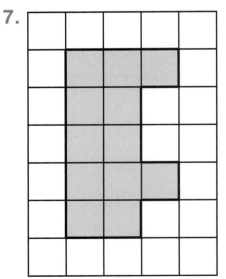

Area = ☐ square centimeters

Count Square Units

1. Which two shapes are congruent?

Shapes _____ and _____ are congruent.

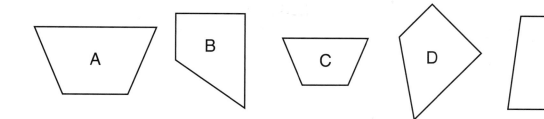

2. Are the two shapes similar? Write similar or not similar.

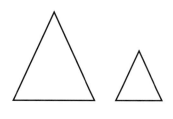

_____

3. Sort these shapes using the rule: quadrilaterals and not quadrilaterals. Write the letters.

The shapes _____ are quadrilaterals.

The shapes _____ are not quadrilaterals.

4. Does the picture show a slide?
   Write yes or no.

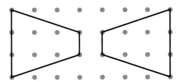

_____

5. Does the picture show a flip over the line?
   Write yes or no.

_____

6. Does the picture show a turn around the point?
   Write yes or no.

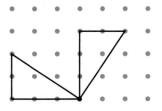

_____

Test

7. Draw the next figure in the pattern.

_____

Find the area in square centimeters.

8.

Area = _____ square centimeters

9.

Area = _____ square centimeters

Name _____

10. **Extended Response** Choose a sorting rule to sort
the shapes into two groups.

My sorting rule is: _____

The shapes _____ are _____.

The shapes _____ are _____.

Test

Dear Family,

In this unit, children will learn different ways to add 3-digit numbers that have totals less than 1,000, with and without regrouping. One way that children will add 3-digit numbers is by counting to 1,000 by tens and by hundreds.

Count to 1,000

Children count by ones from a number, over the hundred, and into the next hundred. For example, 498, 499, 500, 501, 502, 503.

Mistakes often occur when counting this way, so watch for errors that children may make.

Some children will write 5003 instead of 503 for five hundred three. Using Secret Code Cards will help children write the numbers correctly.

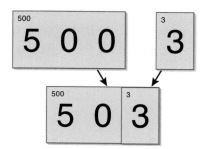

Counting aloud to 1,000 and grouping and labeling small objects provide written and oral practice, and are good ways to help children recognize the difference between 5,003 and 503.

Please call if you have any questions or concerns. Thank you for helping your child learn how to add 3-digit numbers by counting to 1,000.

Sincerely,
Your child's teacher

Carta a la familia

Estimada familia:

En esta unidad los niños están aprendiendo diferentes maneras de sumar números de 3 dígitos con totales de menos de 1,000, reagrupando y sin reagrupar. Una manera en que los niños sumarán números de 3 dígitos es contando hasta 1,000 de diez en diez y de cien en cien.

Contar hasta 1,000

Los niños cuentan de uno en uno a partir de un número, llegan a la centena y comienzan con la siguiente centena.

Por ejemplo, 498, 499, 500, 501, 502, 503.

Cuando se cuenta de esta manera los niños suelen cometer errores. Por lo tanto, preste atención a errores que los niños puedan cometer.

Algunos niños podrian escribir 5003 en vez de 503 al intentar escribir quinientos tres. Usar las Tarjetas de código secreto ayudará a los niños a escribir correctamente los números.

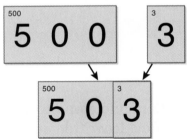

Contar hasta 1,000 en voz alta y poner objectos pequeños en grupos y rotularlos proporcionan práctica oral y escrita, y ayudan a los niños a reconocer la diferencia entre 5,003 y 503.

Si tiene alguna duda o pregunta, por favor comuníquese conmigo. Gracias por ayudar a su niño a aprender a sumar números de 3 dígitos contando hasta 1,000.

Atentamente,
El maestro de su niño

Count Numbers to 1,000

Class Activity

Name _____

Vocabulary

estimate
actual amount

► **Estimate the Number of Objects in a Container**

1. **Estimate** the number of objects.
   Then count the **actual amount**.

Estimate			Actual (Real Amount)		
_____ Groups of 100	_____ Groups of 10	_____ Extra Ones	_____ Groups of 100	_____ Groups of 10	_____ Extra Ones

2. Draw boxes, sticks, and circles to show the
   number of objects the class has.

Groups of 100 (boxes)	Groups of 10 (sticks)	Extra Ones (circles)

3. **On the Back** Use the picture. Estimate to
   find the answer. Then explain how you found
   your estimate.

   Lynn and Ramón picked some apples.
   About how many apples did they pick?

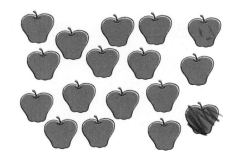

Name _____

▶ Solve and Discuss

Add using any method. Make a proof drawing if it helps.

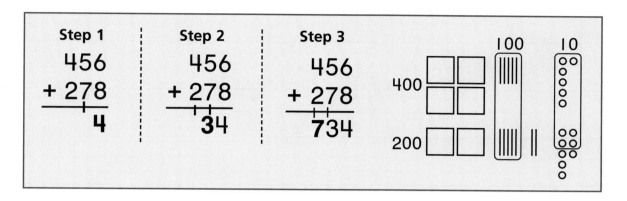

Step 1	Step 2	Step 3
456	456	456
+ 278	+ 278	+ 278
4	34	734

1. 375
   + 482

2. 148
   + 236

3. 584
   + 361

4. 168
   + 674

5. 289
   + 376

6. 563
   + 157

7. 497
   + 259

8. 124
   + 563

9. 348
   + 239

 10. On the Back Write two of your own story problems
   for a classmate to solve.

Name

Solve and Discuss

Dear Family,

Your child is now learning how to add 3-digit numbers. First, children do this with methods they invent themselves or they extend the drawings they did for 2-digit addition.

Children solve the great "mystery" of addition: a hundred can be made from the extra tens, and a ten can be made from the extra ones. *Math Expressions* shows children these two simple methods for 3-digit addition.

New Groups Below

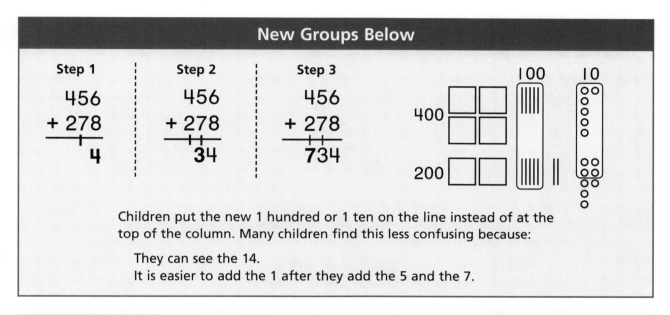

Children put the new 1 hundred or 1 ten on the line instead of at the top of the column. Many children find this less confusing because:

They can see the 14.
It is easier to add the 1 after they add the 5 and the 7.

Show All Totals

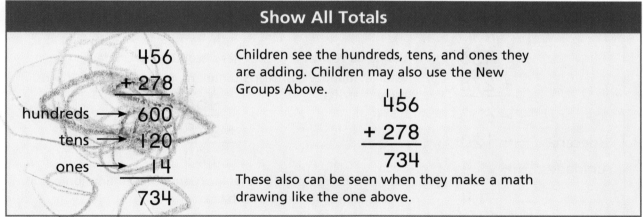

Children see the hundreds, tens, and ones they are adding. Children may also use the New Groups Above.

$$456 + 278 = 734$$

These also can be seen when they make a math drawing like the one above.

Children may use any method that they understand, can explain, and can do fairly quickly. They should use hundreds, tens, and ones language to explain. This shows that they understand that they are adding 4 hundreds and 2 hundreds and not 4 and 2.

Please call if you have questions or comments.

Sincerely,
Your child's teacher

Carta a la familia

Estimada familia:

Ahora su niño está aprendiendo a sumar números de 3 dígitos. Primero, los niños hacen esto con métodos que ellos mismos inventan, o amplílan los dibujos que hicieron para la suma de números de dos dígitos.

Los niños resuelven el "misterio" de la suma: se puede formar una centena a partir de las decenas que sobran y se puede formar una decena a partir de las unidades que sobran. *Math Expressions* les muestra a los niños estos dos métodos simples de suma de números de tres dígitos.

Grupos nuevos abajo

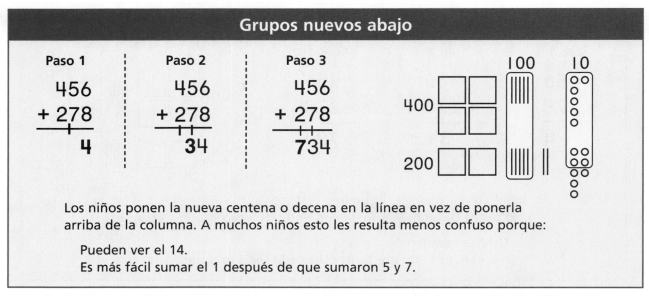

Los niños ponen la nueva centena o decena en la línea en vez de ponerla arriba de la columna. A muchos niños esto les resulta menos confuso porque:

Pueden ver el 14.
Es más fácil sumar el 1 después de que sumaron 5 y 7.

Mostrar todos los totales

$$456$$
$$+278$$
centenas → 600
decenas → 120
unidades → 14
$$734$$

Los niños ven las centenas, las decenas y las unidades que están sumando. Los niños también pueden usar los Grupos nuevos arriba.

$$456$$
$$+278$$
$$734$$

Esto también se puede observar cuando hacen un dibujo matemático como el de arriba.

Los niños pueden usar cualquier método que comprendan, puedan explicar y puedan hacer relativamente rápido. Para explicar deben usar un lenguaje relacionado con centenas, decenas y unidades. Esto demuestra que entienden que están sumando 4 centenas y 2 centenas, y no 4 y 2.

Si tiene alguna duda o pregunta, por favor comuníquese conmigo.

Atentamente,
El maestro de su niño

Solve and Discuss

▶ **Make a Table**

$1.86 Swan	$2.93 Zebra	$4.67 Leopard
$4.96 Bear	$2.68 Raccoon	$3.79 Elephant
$3.79 Kangaroo	$1.55 Owl	$1.58 Turtle
$4.94 Monkey	$2.81 Penguin	$3.57 Giraffe

11–11

Class Activity

► Add 3-Digit Money Amounts

1. Animals: _____

_____

$.

+ $. _____

Make a new ten? _____

Make a new hundred? _____

2. Animals: _____

_____

$.

+ $. _____

Make a new ten? _____

Make a new hundred? _____

3. Animals: _____

_____

$.

+ $. _____

Make a new ten? _____

Make a new hundred? _____

4. Animals: _____

_____

$.

+ $. _____

Make a new ten? _____

Make a new hundred? _____

5. Animals: _____

_____

$.

+ $. _____

Make a new ten? _____

Make a new hundred? _____

6. Animals: _____

_____

$.

+ $. _____

Make a new ten? _____

Make a new hundred? _____

► **Solve and Explain**

Add. Use any method. Make a Proof Drawing if you wish.

1.
```
  2 3 6
+ 4 7 8
```

Make a new ten? _____

Make a new hundred? _____

2. 183 + 517 = _____

Make a new ten? _____

Make a new hundred? _____

3. 93 + 485 = _____

Make a new ten? _____

Make a new hundred? _____

4.
```
  3 6 8
+ 2 5 7
```

Make a new ten? _____

Make a new hundred? _____

5. 347 + 37 = _____

Make a new ten? _____

Make a new hundred? _____

6. 645 + 87 = _____

Make a new ten? _____

Make a new hundred? _____

7. **On the Back** Write and solve a story problem using 3-digit numbers. Explain how you made a new ten or hundred to add the numbers.

Name

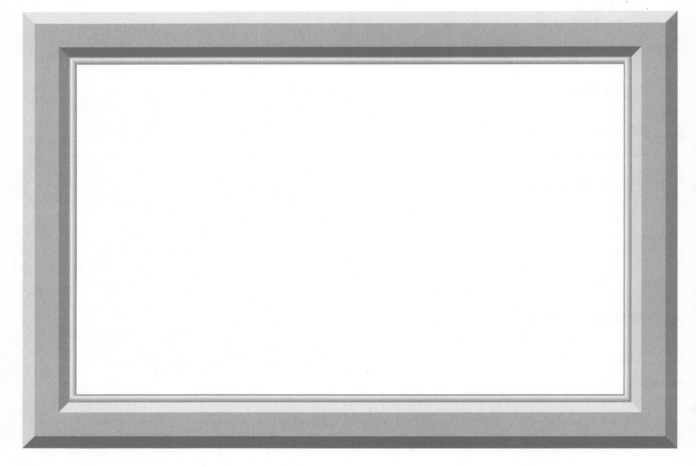

Discuss 3-Digit Addition

Name _____

► **Find the Hidden Animal**

Directions for the puzzle appearing on page 370.

1. Start by coloring in the six dotted squares. These are "free" squares. They are part of the puzzle solution.

2. Solve a problem below. Then look for the answer in the puzzle grid. Color it in.

3. Solve all 20 questions correctly. Color in all 20 correct answers.

4. Name the hidden picture. It is a(n) _____.

524 +247	287 +164	384 +375	456 +174	327 +265

207 +595	248 +376	282 +457	548 +387	233 +288

367 +265	293 +595	284 +376	295 +463	138 +327

286 + 78	407 +266	503 +148	78 +65	192 +339

See page 369 for directions on how to solve the puzzle.

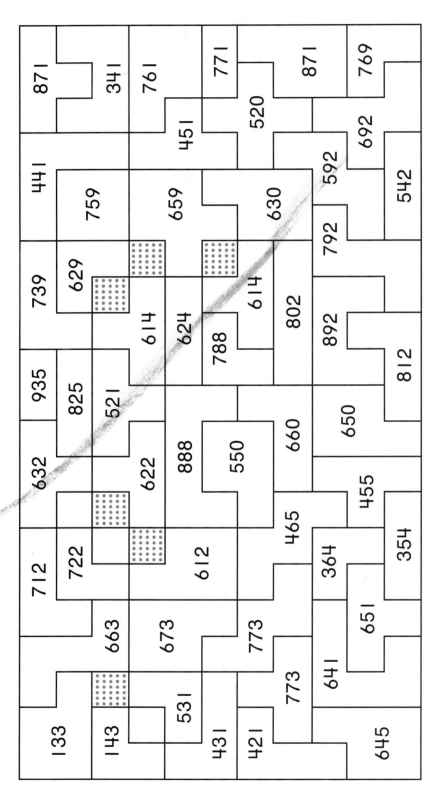

Discuss 3-Digit Addition

► **Adding Up to Solve Story Problems**
Solve each story problem.   **Show your work.**

1. Mr. Cruz planted 750 yams to sell.
   After he sold some, he had 278 yams
   left. How many yams did he sell?

   ☐ _____
              label

2. Last year there were 692 houses in
   our town. This year some new
   houses were built. Now there are
   976 houses. How many new houses
   were built this year?

   ☐ _____
              label

3. Delia had 524 rocks in her collection.
   She gave some to her sister. Then
   she had 462 rocks. How many rocks
   did she give away?

   ☐ _____
              label

4. On Saturday, 703 people went to a
   movie. 194 went in the afternoon.
   The rest went in the evening. How
   many people went in the evening?

   ☐ _____
              label

5. **On the Back** Write a story problem with the answer **235 seashells.**

Story Problems: Unknown Addends

Family Letter

Dear Family,

Your child is now learning how to subtract 3-digit numbers. The most important part is understanding and being able to explain a method. Children may use any method that they understand, can explain, and can perform fairly quickly.

Expanded Method	**Ungroup First Method**

Expanded Method

Step 1

$432 = 400 + 30 + 2$
$-273 = -200 + 70 + 3$

Step 2

$$300 + 120 + 12$$
$$\cancel{400} + \cancel{30} + \cancel{2}$$
$$- 200 + 70 + 3$$

Step 3 $\begin{cases} 100 + 50 + 9 \\ = 159 \end{cases}$

Step 1 "Expand" each number to show that it is made up of hundreds, tens, and ones.

Step 2 Check to see if there are enough ones to subtract from. If not, ungroup a ten into 10 ones and add it to the existing ones. Check to see if there are enough tens to subtract from. If not, ungroup a hundred into 10 tens and add it to the existing tens. Children may also ungroup from the left.

Step 3 Subtract to find the answer. Children may subtract from left to right or right to left.

Ungroup First Method

 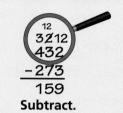

Ungroup from the right.   Subtract.

Step 1 Check to see if there are enough ones and tens to subtract from. Ungroup where needed.

Look inside 432. Ungroup 432 and rename it as 3 hundreds, 12 tens, and 12 ones.

Ungroup from the left:

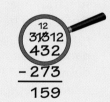

Step 2 Subtract to find the answer. Children may subtract from the left or from the right.

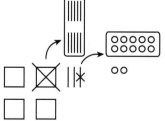

Ungroup

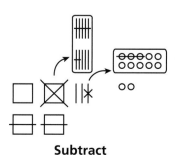

Subtract

In explaining any method they use, children are expected to use "hundreds, tens, and ones" language to show that they understand place value.

Please call if you have questions or comments.

Sincerely,
Your child's teacher

Carta a la familia

Estimada familia:

Su niño está aprendiendo a restar números de 3 dígitos. Lo más importante es comprender y saber explicar un método. Los niños pueden usar cualquier método que comprendan, puedan explicar y puedan hacer relativamente rápido.

Método extendido	Método de desagrupar primero

Método extendido

Paso 1   **Paso 2**

$$300 + 120 + 12$$

$$432 = \quad 400 + 30 + 2 \qquad 400 + 30 + 2$$
$$-273 = \quad -200 + 70 + 3 \qquad -200 + 70 + 3$$

Paso 3 $\begin{cases} 100 + 50 + 9 \\ = 159 \end{cases}$

Paso 1 "Extender" cada número para mostrar que consta de centenas, decenas y unidades.

Paso 2 Observar si hay suficientes unidades para restar. Si no, desagrupar una decena para formar 10 unidades y sumarlas a las unidades existentes. Observar si hay suficientes decenas para restar. Si no, desagrupar una centena para formar 10 decenas y sumarlas a las decenas existentes. Los niños también pueden desagrupar por la izquierda.

Paso 3 Restar para hallar la respuesta. Los niños pueden restar de izquierda a derecha o de derecha a izquierda.

Método de desagrupar primero

Desagrupar por la derecha	**Restar**

Paso 1 Observar si hay suficientes unidades y decenas para restar. Desagrupar cuando haga falta.

Mirar dentro de 432. Desagrupar 432 y volver a nombrarlo como 3 centenas, 12 decenas y 12 unidades.

Desagrupar por la izquierda:

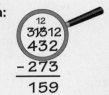

Paso 2 Restar para hallar la respuesta. Los niños pueden restar empezando por la izquierda o por la derecha.

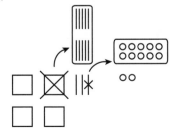

Desagrupar

Para explicar cualquier método que usen, los niños deben usar un lenguaje relacionado con centenas, decenas y unidades para demostrar que comprenden el valor posicional.

Si tiene alguna duda o comentario, por favor comuníquese conmigo.

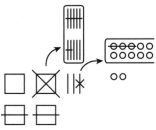

Restar

Atentamente,
El maestro de su niño

Class Activity

Name _____

► **Review Addition and Subtraction**

Ring *add* or *subtract*. Check if you need to ungroup or
make a new ten or hundred. Then find the answer.

1. 7 6 2
   − 3 9 5
   _____

Subtract

☐ Ungroup to get 10 ones

☐ Ungroup to get 10 tens

Add

☐ Make 1 new ten

☐ Make 1 new hundred

2. 3 9 5
   + 3 6 7
   _____

Subtract

☐ Ungroup to get 10 ones

☐ Ungroup to get 10 tens

Add

☐ Make 1 new ten

☐ Make 1 new hundred

3. 2 8 7
   − 1 9 3
   _____

Subtract

☐ Ungroup to get 10 ones

☐ Ungroup to get 10 tens

Add

☐ Make 1 new ten

☐ Make 1 new hundred

4. 4 3 7
   + 3 2 4
   _____

Subtract

☐ Ungroup to get 10 ones

☐ Ungroup to get 10 tens

Add

☐ Make 1 new ten

☐ Make 1 new hundred

5. On the Back Explain how you know when to ungroup
in subtraction. Use the words *ones*, *tens*, and *hundreds*.

Name _____

_____

_____

_____

_____

_____

_____

_____

_____

_____

_____

_____

_____

_____

_____

_____

_____

Relationships between Addition and Subtraction Methods

Name _____

► **Solve and Discuss**

Solve each story problem.

1. Lucero spilled a bag of marbles. 219 fell on the floor. 316 were still in the bag. How many were in the bag before it spilled?

☐ _____
label

2. Al counted bugs in the park. He counted 561 on Monday. He counted 273 fewer than that on Tuesday. How many bugs did he count on both days combined?

☐ _____
label

3. Happy the Clown gives out balloons. She gave out 285 at the zoo and then she gave out some more at the amusement park. Altogether she gave out 503. How many balloons did she give out at the amusement park?

☐ _____
label

4. Charlie the Clown gave out 842 balloons at the fun fair. He gave out 194 at the store. He gave out 367 at the playground. How many more balloons did he give out at the fun fair than at the playground?

☐ _____
label

▶ **Practice Story Problems**

Solve. Show your work on a separate sheet of paper.

1. Damon collects stamps. He had 383 stamps. Then he bought 126 more at a yard sale. How many stamps does he have now?

```
┌──────────┐
│          │  _____
└──────────┘
   label
```

2. Mr. Lewis sold 438 melons yesterday. Now he has 294 melons left to sell. How many melons did he have to start?

```
┌──────────┐
│          │  _____
└──────────┘
   label
```

3. Ali is passing out ribbons for a race. She passed out 57 ribbons so far and she has 349 ribbons left. How many ribbons did she have at the start?

```
┌──────────┐
│          │  _____
└──────────┘
   label
```

4. Tanya is doing a puzzle. She has put together 643 pieces. There are 1,000 pieces in the puzzle. How many pieces are left to put together?

```
┌──────────┐
│          │  _____
└──────────┘
   label
```

5. Pawel passed out fliers to advertise a play. He passed out 194 fliers at the bakery. He passed out 358 at the grocery store. How many more fliers did he pass out at the grocery store than at the bakery?

```
┌──────────┐
│          │  _____
└──────────┘
   label
```

6. Cora collected 542 sports cards last year. She collected 247 fewer than that this year. How many cards did she collect in both years together?

```
┌──────────┐
│          │  _____
└──────────┘
   label
```

Mixed Addition and Subtraction Story Problems

Class Activity

Name _____

► **The Yard Sale**

Choose any two toys to buy. Pay for them with $10.00.

$4.87	$3.49	$2.59	$1.64
Baseball Glove	Globe	Perfume	Funny Glasses
$1.55	$2.48	$4.86	$3.97
Toy Binoculars	Toy Lamb	Ring	Toy Guitar

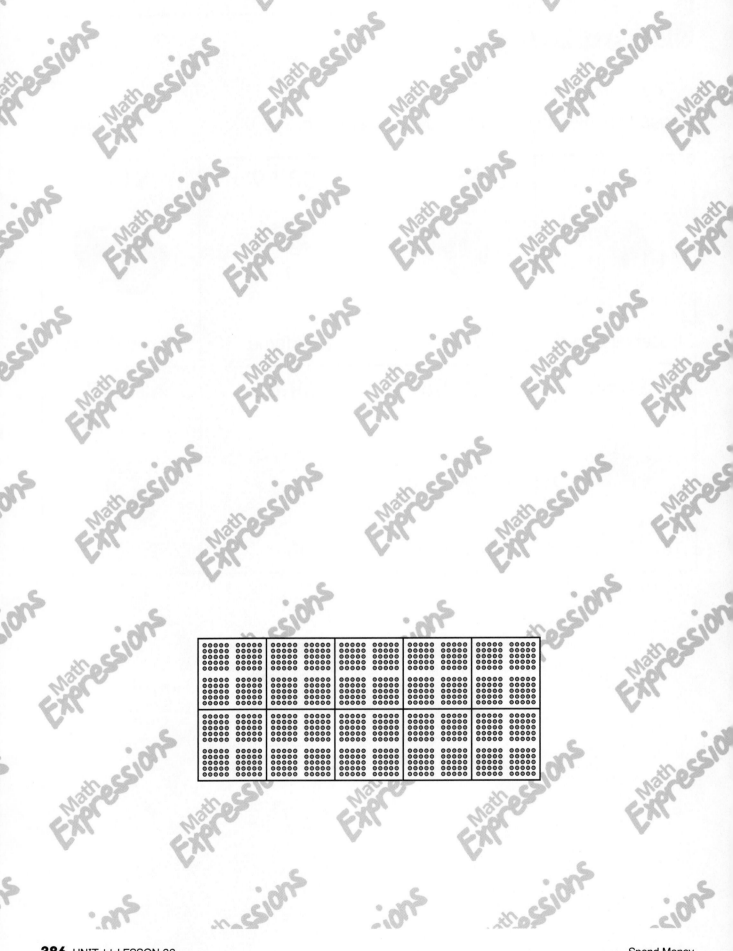

Spend Money

Subtract.

18.   5 0 5
    − 3 7 1
    _____

19.   3 0 0
    − 2 3 9
    _____

20. $ 1 0 . 0 0
    − $ 4 . 8 1
    _____

21. $10.00 − $2.72 = _____

Solve.   Show your work.

22. Dena picked 472 apples. She sold
    187 at the Farmers Market. How
    many apples did she have left?

    [   ] _____
                    label

23. This morning 256 books were
    returned to the library. 596 more
    were returned this afternoon.
    How many books were returned
    altogether?

    [   ] _____
                    label

Solve.   **Show your work.**

24. Ada read 124 pages in a book. The book has 300 pages. How many more pages does she still have to read to finish the book?

```
┌──────────┐
│          │  _____
└──────────┘        label
```

25. **Extended Response** Write and solve an addition or subtraction story problem using the numbers 458 and 279.

_____

_____

_____

_____

_____

_____

_____

_____

_____

_____

25↑	50↑	75↑	100↑
24	49	74	99
23	48	73	98
22	47	72	97
21	46	71	96
20	45	70	95
19	44	69	94
18	43	68	93
17	42	67	92
16	41	66	91
15	40	65	90
14	39	64	89
13	38	63	88
12	37	62	87
11	36	61	86
10	35	60	85
9	34	59	84
8	33	58	83
7	32	57	82
6	31	56	81
5	30	55	80
4	29	54	79
3	28	53	78
2	27	52	77
1	26	51	76
	25↓	50↓	75↓

50 100 20 70 40 90 10 30 60 80

Step 1: Cut out on the dashed lines.

Step 2: Put the sections in order.

Step 3: Tape or paste the sections together.

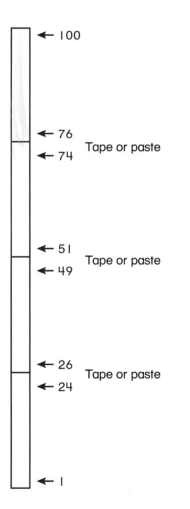

← 100

← 76
← 74   Tape or paste

← 51
← 49   Tape or paste

← 26
← 24   Tape or paste

← 1

Meter Stick

Class Activity

Name _____

► **Estimate and Measure**

Find a part of your hand that is about the length of each measure.

1. 1 cm _____

2. 1 dm _____

Find a part of your body that is about 1 meter long.

3. 1 m _____

Find the real object. Estimate and measure its length.
Round if necessary.

4.

Estimate: about _____ cm

Measure: _____ cm

5.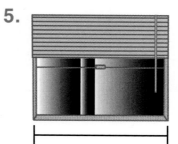

Estimate: about _____ cm

Measure: _____ cm

6.

Estimate: about _____ dm

Measure: _____ dm

7.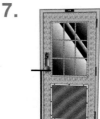

Estimate: about _____ m

Measure: _____ m

Draw a line segment to show each length.

8. 1 cm

9. 1 dm

Name _____

Class Activity

▶ Measure Heights

When you measure a length greater than 1 m, you place two meter sticks end-to-end. The first meter stick is 100 cm. You add 100 to the number of centimeters you read from the second meter stick.

10. Complete the table for each person in your group.

Person's Name	Estimated Height (cm)	Actual Height (cm)	Difference Between Estimated and Actual Height (cm)

Use the data you collected to answer these questions.

11. Who is the tallest person in your group?

_____

12. How much taller is the tallest person than the

shortest person? _____

13. Whose estimated height was closest to his or her

actual height? _____

14. On a separate sheet of paper, write four more questions you could ask about this data. Trade your questions with another group and answer each other's questions.

Meters and Decimeters

Dear Family,

In this geometry unit, your child will measure in centimeters, meters, and decimeters. Children develop a sense of the size of each metric unit by finding personal or body referents, drawing line segments, and measuring objects and distances with a meter stick.

Children compare the metric units for length to the U.S. monetary system, both of which use the base ten number system.

1 decimeter = 10 centimeters   1 dime = 10 cents
1 meter = 10 decimeters   1 dollar = 10 dimes
1 meter = 100 centimeters   1 dollar = 100 cents

Children convert units of linear measurement and units of the monetary system. They solve story problems to strengthen their understanding of the base ten system, while reinforcing their skills in the addition of 3-digit numbers.

The last two lessons of this unit introduce children to three-dimensional shapes. They use unit cubes to build rectangular prisms, and they draw these prisms from the top, side, and front view. They also learn how to find the volume of a three-dimensional shape by counting unit cubes.

In the last lesson, children look at attributes of three-dimensional shapes, like vertices, faces, and edges.

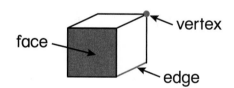

Children also investigate how different three-dimensional shapes stack and if they roll or slide across a surface. They then sort three-dimensional shapes by attributes.

If you have any questions or comments, please call or write to me.

Sincerely,
Your child's teacher

Estimada familia:

En esta unidad sobre geometría, su niño medirá con centímetros, metros y decímetros. Los niños van a comprender el tamaño de cada unidad métrica usando el cuerpo como punto de referencia, dibujando segmentos de recta y midiendo objetos y distancias con una regla de un metro.

Los niños van a comparar las unidades métricas de longitud con el sistema monetario de los EE. UU., ya que ambos utilizan el sistema de base diez.

1 decímetro = 10 centímetros	1 moneda de 10¢ = 10 centavos
1 metro = 10 decímetros	1 dólar = 10 monedas de 10¢
1 metro = 100 centímetros	1 dólar = 100 centavos

Los niños van a convertir unidades de longitud y unidades del sistema monetario. También resolverán problemas para reforzar su comprensión del sistema de base diez, a la vez que refuerzan su habilidad de sumar números de 3 dígitos.

Las dos últimas lecciones de esta unidad presentan las figuras tridimensionales. Los niños usarán cubos de unidad para construir prismas rectangulares y dibujarán los prismas desde arriba, desde el lado y desde adelante. También aprenderán cómo se calcula el volumen de una figura tridimensional contando cubos de unidad.

En la última lección, los niños estudiar los atributos de figuras tridimensionales tales como vértices, caras y aristas.

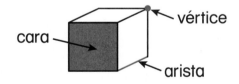

También verán cómo se pueden apilar las figuras tridimensionales y si ruedan o se deslizan sobre una superficie. Luego clasificarán las figuras tridimensionales según sus atributos.

Si tiene alguna duda o comentario, por favor comuníquese conmigo.

Atentamente,
El maestro de su niño

Meters and Decimeters

Class Activity

▶ Guessing Game

In this game, you and a partner will write clues that describe rectangular objects in the classroom. You will trade clues with another pair and try to find their objects.

Step 1: Measure the length and width of 3 objects. Record your measurements in the table below.

Object Dimensions		
Object	**Length (cm)**	**Width (cm)**

Step 2: Write 2 clues that describe each object.
Clue 1: Write the object's length and width.
Clue 2: Describe the object by color, location, shape, or use.
Step 3: Write the name of the object on the back of the index card.

What Am I?
Clue 1: I am 67 cm long and 44 cm wide.
Clue 2: I usually hang on the wall at the front of the classroom.

Answer

bulletin board

Step 4: Read your clues to another pair. Ask them to guess each of your objects by first estimating and then measuring to check.

Class Activity

► **Penny Toss Game**

In this game, you will stand at the start line and toss a penny as close as possible to the goal line.

Step 1:	Take turns tossing a penny as close as possible to the goal line.
Step 2:	Measure the distance of your toss in centimeters from the goal line.
Step 3:	Complete the table below.

Penny Toss Game	
Name	**Distance from the goal line (cm)**

14. Whose penny landed closest to the goal line?

_____

15. How many children's pennies landed less than 10 cm from the goal line? _____

16. On a separate sheet of paper, write three more comparison questions about the data you collected. Share your questions with the group and answer them together.

Class Activity

Name _____

▶ **Money and Length Equivalencies**

Answer each question. Draw a picture if you need to.

1. How many ones in

   I ten? _____

2. How many dimes in

   I dollar? _____

3. How many pennies in

   I dime? _____

4. How many tens in

   I hundred? _____

5. How many centimeters in

   I dm? _____

6. How many cents in

   I dime? _____

7. How many pennies in

   I dollar? _____

8. How many ones in

   I hundred? _____

9. Write the numbers.

5 m 8 dm 4 cm	_____ m _____ dm _____ cm
= _____ dm 4 cm	= 41 dm 2 cm
= _____ cm	= _____ cm
$3.18	$ _____
= _____ dimes _____ pennies	= _____ dimes _____ pennies
= _____ pennies	= 412 pennies

10. **On the Back** Draw a picture to show the relationship between metric lengths (meters, decimeters, centimeters) and money (dollars, dimes, pennies).

Name

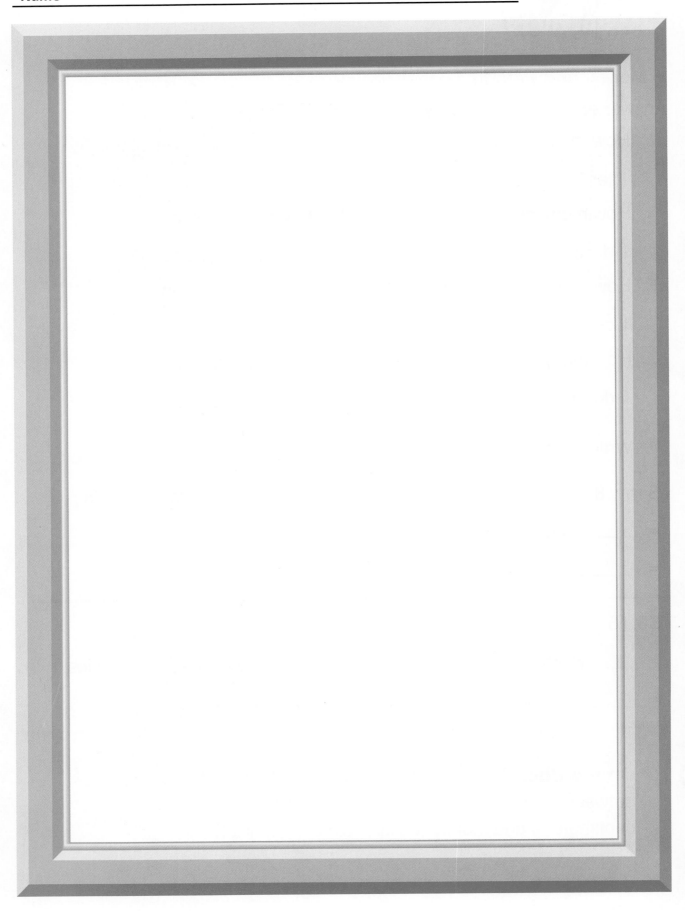

Practice with Meters and Money

Class Activity

▶ **Rectangular Prisms**

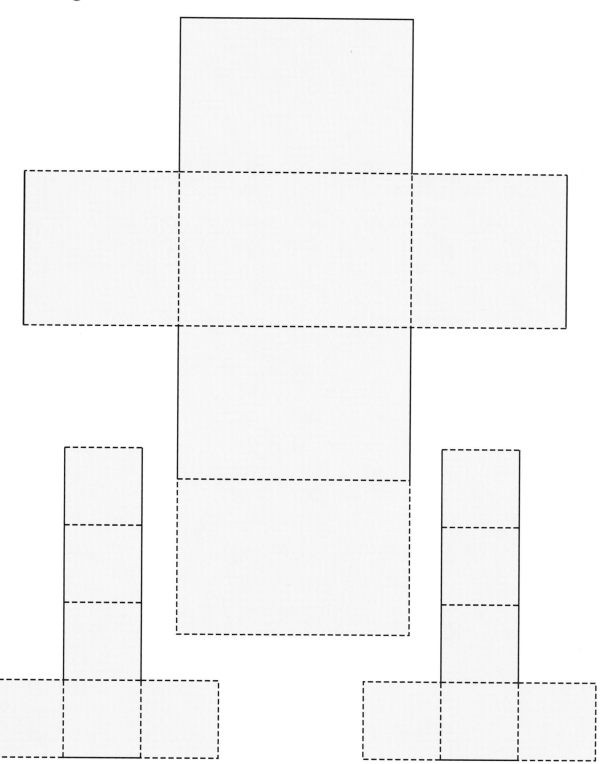

Cut on solid lines.

Fold on dashed lines.

Rectangular Prisms

Class Activity

Vocabulary
rectangular prism
views

▶ Build and Draw Rectangular Prisms

Using unit cubes, build a **rectangular prism** to match each description. Draw the rectangular prism from the top, front, and side **views**.

1. two rows of three unit cubes

| **top view** | **front view** | **side view** |

2. one row of two unit cubes stacked on top of another row of two unit cubes

| **top view** | **front view** | **side view** |

▶ Build Rectangular Prisms from Drawings

Build a rectangular prism to match each set of views.

3.

| **top view** | **front view** | **side view** |

4.

| **top view** | **front view** | **side view** |

Class Activity

Name _____

Vocabulary

volume
cubic units

▶ **Volume of 3-Dimensional Shapes**

The **volume** of a 3-dimensional shape is the amount of space it occupies.

To measure volume, you can find the number of **cubic units** that make up the 3-dimensional shape.

I cubic unit

Find the volume of each shape in cubic units.

5.

_____ cubic units

6.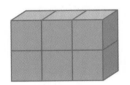

_____ cubic units

7.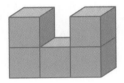

_____ cubic units

8.

_____ cubic units

9.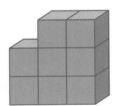

_____ cubic units

10.

_____ cubic units

Use unit cubes to build each 3-dimensional shape.
Find the volume by counting cubic units.

11.

_____ cubic units

12.

_____ cubic units

13.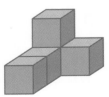

_____ cubic units

Write the numbers.

1. 170 cm = _____ m _____ dm

2. 654 cm = _____ m _____ dm _____ cm

3. 575 cm = _____ m _____ dm _____ cm

Is each shape **2-D (two-dimensional)** or
3-D (three-dimensional)?

4.  _____

5. _____

6. Draw the top, front, and side views.

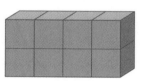

Top View   **Front View**   **Side View**

Find the volume of each shape in cubic units.

7.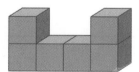

_____ cubic units

8.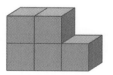

_____ cubic units

9. Sort the shapes. Write the names of the shapes in the Venn diagram.

cube

sphere

cylinder

cone

rectangular prism

square pyramid

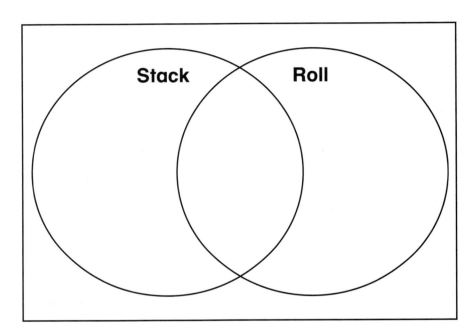

10. **Extended Response** Explain how knowing about ones, tens, and hundreds can help you write 138 centimeters as meters, decimeters, and centimeters.

_____

_____

_____

_____

_____

Test

Name _____

▶ **Practice Multiplication**

I have 5 vases. There are 2 flowers in each vase.

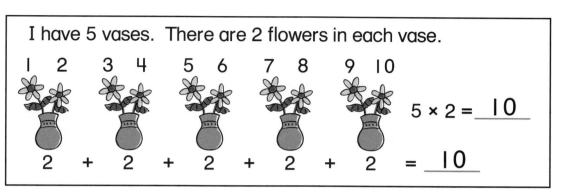

$5 \times 2 =$ __10__

2 + 2 + 2 + 2 + 2 = __10__

Write the addition and **multiplication** equation for each story. Make a math drawing to help you solve the problem.

---

1. I have 4 cats. Each cat has 3 toy mice. How many mice are there?

$3 + 3 + 3 + 3 =$ _____

$4 \times 3 =$ _____

[ ] _____
    label

---

2. I eat 4 pieces of fruit every day. How many pieces of fruit do I eat in 5 days?

___ + ___ + ___ + ___ + ___ = _____

$5 \times 4 =$ _____

[ ] _____
    label

---

3. I have 3 packs of pencils. There are 5 pencils in each pack. How many pencils do I have?

$5 + 5 + 5 =$ _____

_____ × _____ = _____

[ ] _____
    label

▶ **2s Count-Bys**

Ring each pair.

4. Fill in the chart below to make groups of 2. Ring each pair.
Then **count by** 2s by saying the last number in each group.

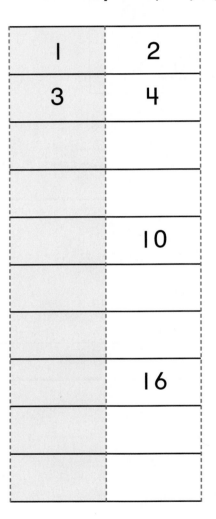

1	2
3	4
	10
	16

5. Write out the 2s **count-bys** below.

 2   4   ___   ___   10   ___   ___   16   ___

Introduction to Multiplication

Dear Family,

In this unit, children are introduced to multiplication in three ways.

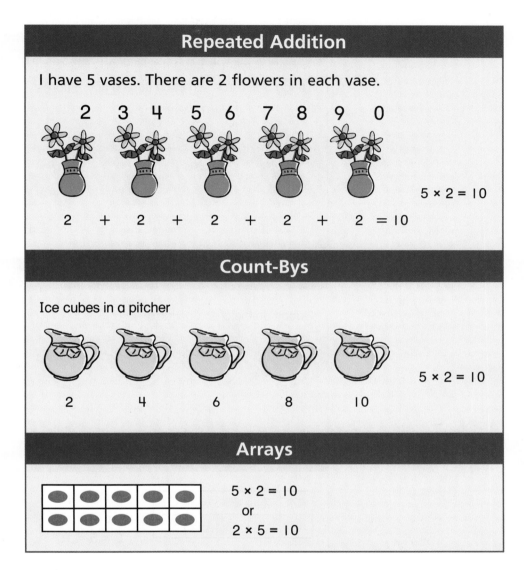

Repeated Addition

I have 5 vases. There are 2 flowers in each vase.

2   3   4   5   6   7   8   9   0

$2 + 2 + 2 + 2 + 2 = 10$

$5 \times 2 = 10$

Count-Bys

Ice cubes in a pitcher

2   4   6   8   10

$5 \times 2 = 10$

Arrays

$5 \times 2 = 10$
or
$2 \times 5 = 10$

Please call if you have any questions or comments. Thank you for helping your child learn about multiplication.

Sincerely,
Your child's teacher

Estimada familia:

En esta unidad se la multiplicación de tres maneras.

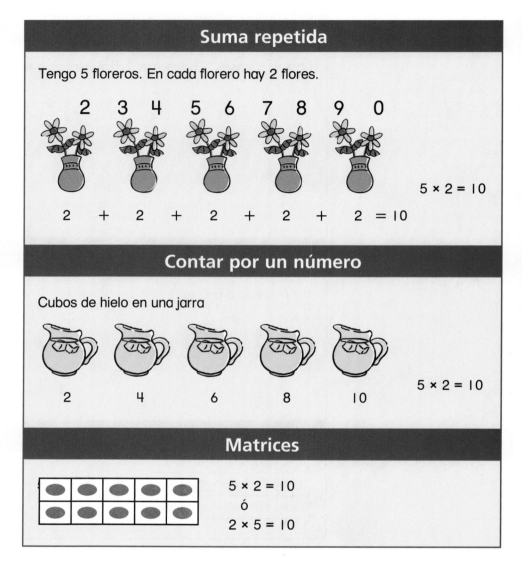

Suma repetida

Tengo 5 floreros. En cada florero hay 2 flores.

2 3 4 5 6 7 8 9 0

$5 \times 2 = 10$

2 + 2 + 2 + 2 + 2 = 10

Contar por un número

Cubos de hielo en una jarra

2   4   6   8   10

$5 \times 2 = 10$

Matrices

$5 \times 2 = 10$
ó
$2 \times 5 = 10$

Si tiene alguna duda o comentario, por favor comuníquese conmigo. Gracias por ayudar a su niño a aprender sobre la multiplicación.

Atentamente,
El maestro de su niño

Introduction to Multiplication

Going Further

▶ Using Pictographs

Use the pictograph to answer the questions.

Playground Toys

Soccer balls	☆ ☆ ☆
Jump ropes	☆ ☆ ☆ ☆
Bats	☆ ☆

Key: Each ☆ = 4 toys

1. How many jump ropes are there in all?

label

2. How many more soccer balls are there than bats?

label

3. A school has 8 tennis rackets. How many ☆s are needed to show the tennis rackets in this pictograph?

label

4. **On the Back** How many ☆s are needed to show the soccer balls if each ☆ represents 2 toys? Write the answer and show your work on the back.

Class Activity

Name

Vocabulary
count by
count-bys

▶ **5s Count-Bys**

1. Fill in the chart below to make groups of 5. Then **count by** 5s by saying the last number in each group.

1	2	3	4	5
6	7	8	9	10
	17			
				25
		33		

2. Write out the 5s **count-bys** below.

__5__ ____ ____ ____ __25__ ____ ____ ____ ____ ____

Name _____

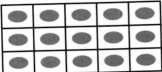

▶ **Solve Array Problems.**

Write the numbers.

3.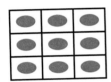

_____ × _____ or

_____ × _____

4.

_____ × _____ or

_____ × _____

5.

_____ × _____

6.

_____ × _____ or

_____ × _____

Plant some beans in your garden.
Your teacher will tell you how.

7.

Groups of Five and Array

Class Activity

Name _____

Vocabulary

count-bys
multiplication

▶ Use Arrays to Solve Problems

Here is Mr. and Mrs. Green's orchard.

1. How many apple trees are in the orchard?
   Write the **count-bys** and the **multiplication.**
   Count by 5s.

   <u> 5 </u> <u> 10 </u> _____ _____ _____ _____ _____ _____

   <u> 8 </u> × _____ = _____

2. Count by 8s.

   <u> 8 </u> <u> 16 </u> _____ _____ _____

   <u> 5 </u> × _____ = _____

Going Further

Name _____

Vocabulary

array

▶ Introduce Mystery Multiplication

You can use an **array** to find the unknown number
in a multiplication sentence.

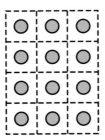

1. How many rows are there in the array? [ ]

_____
label

2. How many columns are there in the array? [ ]

_____
label

3. How many circles are there in all? [ ]

_____
label

4. Complete the multiplication sentence.

[ ] × 3 = 12

Find the unknown number in each multiplication
sentence. Place beans on the grid to make an array to
help you.

5. 5 × [ ] = 20

6. 4 × [ ] = 8

7. [ ] × 2 = 10

8. [ ] × 3 = 9

Work with Arrays

Class Activity

Name _____

▶ **Solve and Discuss**

Draw in your answers. Write the numbers.

1. Kathy has **half** as many marbles as Yao.

   Kathy has _____.

   Yao has _____.

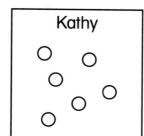

2. Paulo and Leah have **equal shares** of blocks.

   Paulo has _____.

   Leah has _____.

3. Nicole has **twice** as many stickers as Reggie.

   Nicole has _____.

   Reggie has _____.

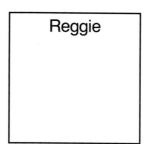
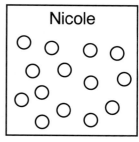

4. Dean has **double** the number of stamps that Yolanda has.

   Yolanda has _____.

   Dean has _____.

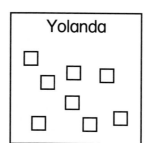

5. **On the Back** Draw a picture to show equal shares of 14. Explain how you know your picture shows equal shares.

Name _____

Use counters to model each problem.

1. Pedro has 16 cards. How can he share the cards equally with Erik, Dana, and Audrey? Draw a picture.

You can **divide** 16 cards into 4 groups of 4.

2. There are 20 markers. There are 5 friends. How can they share the markers equally?

   _____ groups of _____

3. There are 16 marbles in a jar. How can Nick and Warrick share the marbles equally?

   _____ groups of _____

4. There are 24 stickers. There are 3 children. How can they share the stickers equally?

   _____ groups of _____

5. Use 12 counters. Show different ways you can make equal groups.

Class Activity

> **Vocabulary**
>
> repeated subtraction

Solve. Use **repeated subtraction.**

1. How many times can you subtract 3 from 15?

   The number of times you can subtract 3 is _____.

   $15 \div 3 =$ _____

   $15 - 3 =$ _____

   _____ $- 3 =$ _____

   _____ $- 3 =$ _____

   _____ $- 3 =$ _____

   _____ $- 3 =$ _____

---

2. How many times can you subtract 2 from 14?

   The number of times you can subtract 2 is _____.

   $14 \div 2 =$ _____

   $14 - 2 =$ _____

   _____ $- 2 =$ _____

   _____ $- 2 =$ _____

   _____ $- 2 =$ _____

   _____ $- 2 =$ _____

   _____ $- 2 =$ _____

   _____ $- 2 =$ _____

---

3. $9 \div 3 =$ _____

4. $20 \div 4 =$ _____

5. $12 \div 3 =$ _____

6. $15 \div 5 =$ _____

7. $21 \div 3 =$ _____

8. $18 \div 6 =$ _____

Model Division

Name _____

Class Activity

Vocabulary
line of symmetry

▶ Complete Drawings of Symmetrical Shapes

Finish drawing the shapes.

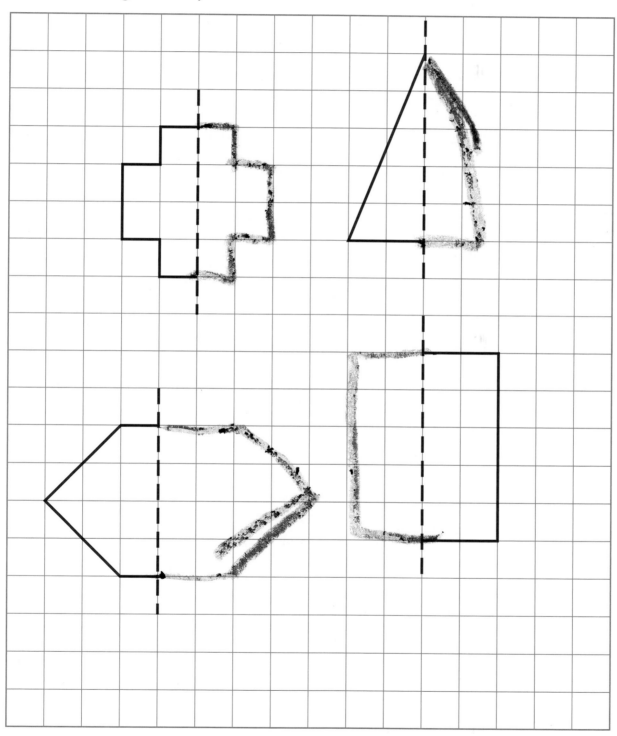

On the Back Draw some symmetrical shapes of your own. Draw a **line of symmetry** for each shape.

Name _____

Class Activity

▶ **Shade Unit Fractions**

I. Shade in the fractions for the shapes.

$\frac{1}{2}$

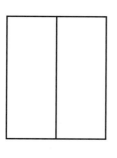
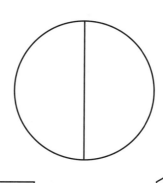
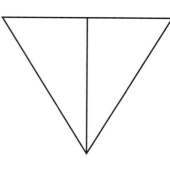

$\frac{1}{3}$

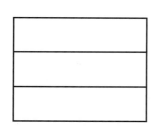
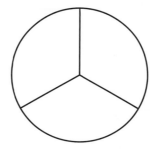
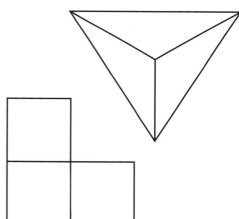

$\frac{1}{4}$

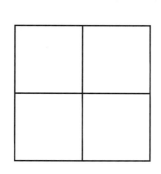
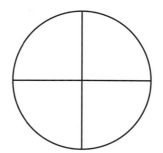
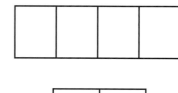

▶ **Shade and Write Fractions**

2. Shade in the fractions for the shapes.

$\frac{1}{2}$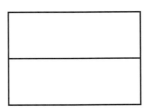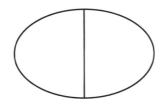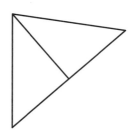

$\frac{2}{3} = \frac{1}{3} + \frac{1}{3}$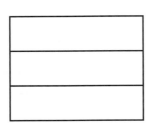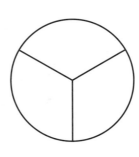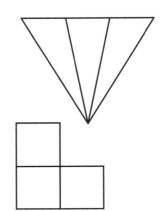

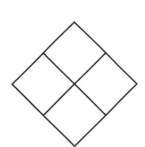 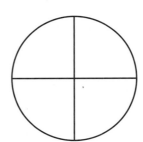 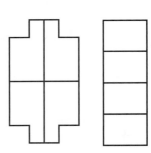

$\frac{3}{4} = \frac{1}{4} + \frac{1}{4} + \frac{1}{4}$

How much is shaded? Write the fraction.

3. 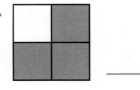 _____

4. 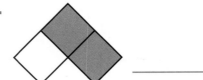 _____

► **Divide Shapes Into Equal Parts**

Shade in the fractions of the shapes.

5.

$$\frac{1}{2}$$

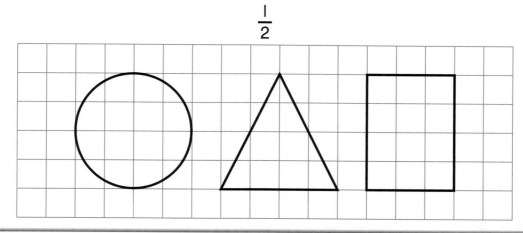

6.

$$\frac{2}{3} = \frac{1}{3} + \frac{1}{3}$$

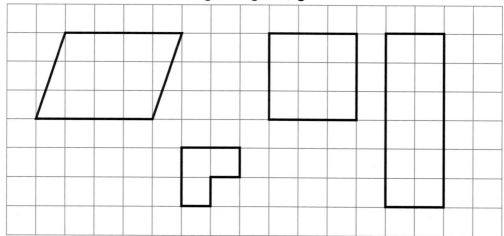

7.

$$\frac{3}{4} = \frac{1}{4} + \frac{1}{4} + \frac{1}{4}$$

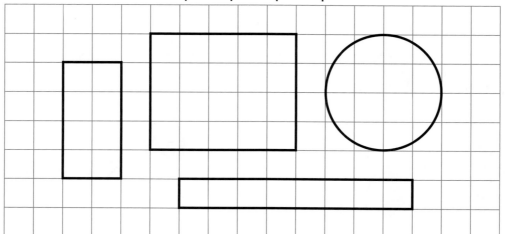

Going Further

Name _____

► **Solve and Discuss**

Color to show each fraction.

1. $\dfrac{1}{5}$

2. $\dfrac{4}{6} = \dfrac{1}{6} + \dfrac{1}{6} + \dfrac{1}{6} + \dfrac{1}{6}$

3. $\dfrac{3}{7} = \dfrac{1}{7} + \dfrac{1}{7} + \dfrac{1}{7}$

4. $\dfrac{2}{8} = \dfrac{1}{8} + \dfrac{1}{8}$

5. $\dfrac{3}{10} = \dfrac{1}{10} + \dfrac{1}{10} + \dfrac{1}{10}$

6. $\dfrac{2}{9} = \dfrac{1}{9} + \dfrac{1}{9}$

Write the fraction for the shaded part.

7.

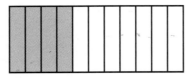

8.

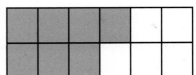

9.

10.

11.

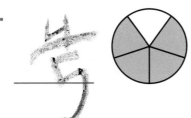

12.

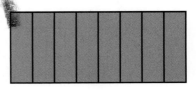

Fractions

Class Activity

► **Make Fraction Strips**

Color the fraction strips. Cut on the dashed lines.

1. Color 1 whole.	I whole
2. Color $\frac{1}{2}$.	$\frac{1}{2}$ $\frac{1}{2}$
3. Color $\frac{1}{3}$.	$\frac{1}{3}$ $\frac{1}{3}$ $\frac{1}{3}$
4. Color $\frac{2}{3}$. $\frac{2}{3} = \frac{1}{3} + \frac{1}{3}$	$\frac{1}{3}$ $\frac{1}{3}$ $\frac{1}{3}$
5. Color $\frac{1}{4}$.	$\frac{1}{4}$ $\frac{1}{4}$ $\frac{1}{4}$ $\frac{1}{4}$
6. Color $\frac{2}{4}$. $\frac{2}{4} = \frac{1}{4} + \frac{1}{4}$	$\frac{1}{4}$ $\frac{1}{4}$ $\frac{1}{4}$ $\frac{1}{4}$
7. Color $\frac{3}{4}$. $\frac{3}{4} = \frac{1}{4} + \frac{1}{4} + \frac{1}{4}$	$\frac{1}{4}$ $\frac{1}{4}$ $\frac{1}{4}$ $\frac{1}{4}$

More on Fractions

Name _____

▶ Compare Fractions

Use your fraction strips to compare the
fractions. Then write <, >, or =.

Remember
> means is greater than.
< means is less than.
= means is equal to.

8. Compare $\frac{1}{3}$ and $\frac{1}{2}$.

$\frac{1}{3}$ ◯ $\frac{1}{2}$

9. Compare $\frac{2}{4}$ and $\frac{3}{4}$.

$\frac{2}{4}$ ◯ $\frac{3}{4}$

10. Compare $\frac{2}{3}$ and $\frac{1}{3}$.

$\frac{2}{3}$ ◯ $\frac{1}{3}$

11. Compare $\frac{1}{4}$ and $\frac{1}{2}$.

$\frac{1}{4}$ ◯ $\frac{1}{2}$

12. Compare $\frac{3}{4}$ and $\frac{2}{3}$.

$\frac{3}{4}$ ◯ $\frac{2}{3}$

13. Compare $\frac{2}{3}$ and $\frac{1}{2}$.

$\frac{2}{3}$ ◯ $\frac{1}{2}$

14. Compare $\frac{2}{4}$ and $\frac{1}{2}$.

$\frac{2}{4}$ ◯ $\frac{1}{2}$

15. Compare $\frac{2}{3}$ and $\frac{2}{4}$.

$\frac{2}{3}$ ◯ $\frac{2}{4}$

▶ Visual Thinking

Ring the picture that shows the correct amount.

16. less than $\frac{1}{2}$

17. more than $\frac{1}{2}$

Name

▶ Write Money in Different Ways

Complete the chart.

	Money Amount	Number of Cents	Dollars and Cents	Fraction of a Dollar
18.	1 dime	10¢	$0.10	$\frac{1}{10}$
19.	2 dimes	20¢	$0._____	$\frac{}{10}$
20.	3 dimes	_____¢	$0._____	$\frac{}{10}$
21.	6 dimes	60¢	$_____	_____
22.	8 dimes	80¢	$_____	_____
23.	10 dimes	_____¢	$1.00	_____ or 1
24.	1 penny	1¢	$0.01	$\frac{1}{100}$
25.	2 pennies	2¢	$_____	$\frac{}{100}$
26.	8 pennies	_____¢	$_____	$\frac{}{100}$
27.	35 pennies	35¢	$_____	$\frac{}{100}$
28.	80 pennies	_____¢	$0.80	_____
29.	100 pennies	100¢	$_____	_____ or 1

More on Fractions

Name _____

► **Estimate Fractions**

Cut on the dashed lines.

| 0 | $\frac{1}{2}$ | 1 |

| $\frac{1}{2}$ | $\frac{1}{2}$ |

| $\frac{1}{3}$ | $\frac{1}{3}$ | $\frac{1}{3}$ |

| $\frac{1}{4}$ | $\frac{1}{4}$ | $\frac{1}{4}$ | $\frac{1}{4}$ |

| $\frac{1}{5}$ | $\frac{1}{5}$ | $\frac{1}{5}$ | $\frac{1}{5}$ | $\frac{1}{5}$ |

| $\frac{1}{6}$ | $\frac{1}{6}$ | $\frac{1}{6}$ | $\frac{1}{6}$ | $\frac{1}{6}$ | $\frac{1}{6}$ |

| $\frac{1}{7}$ | $\frac{1}{7}$ | $\frac{1}{7}$ | $\frac{1}{7}$ | $\frac{1}{7}$ | $\frac{1}{7}$ | $\frac{1}{7}$ |

| $\frac{1}{8}$ | $\frac{1}{8}$ | $\frac{1}{8}$ | $\frac{1}{8}$ | $\frac{1}{8}$ | $\frac{1}{8}$ | $\frac{1}{8}$ | $\frac{1}{8}$ |

| $\frac{1}{9}$ | $\frac{1}{9}$ | $\frac{1}{9}$ | $\frac{1}{9}$ | $\frac{1}{9}$ | $\frac{1}{9}$ | $\frac{1}{9}$ | $\frac{1}{9}$ | $\frac{1}{9}$ |

| $\frac{1}{10}$ | $\frac{1}{10}$ | $\frac{1}{10}$ | $\frac{1}{10}$ | $\frac{1}{10}$ | $\frac{1}{10}$ | $\frac{1}{10}$ | $\frac{1}{10}$ | $\frac{1}{10}$ | $\frac{1}{10}$ |

| $\frac{1}{11}$ | $\frac{1}{11}$ | $\frac{1}{11}$ | $\frac{1}{11}$ | $\frac{1}{11}$ | $\frac{1}{11}$ | $\frac{1}{11}$ | $\frac{1}{11}$ | $\frac{1}{11}$ | $\frac{1}{11}$ | $\frac{1}{11}$ |

| $\frac{1}{12}$ | $\frac{1}{12}$ | $\frac{1}{12}$ | $\frac{1}{12}$ | $\frac{1}{12}$ | $\frac{1}{12}$ | $\frac{1}{12}$ | $\frac{1}{12}$ | $\frac{1}{12}$ | $\frac{1}{12}$ | $\frac{1}{12}$ | $\frac{1}{12}$ |

On the Back Write the fractions in order from greatest to least. Then write them from least to greatest.

More on Fractions **451**

More on Fractions

Name _____

Class Activity

▶ **The Spinner Game**

Color the larger part of the spinner blue. 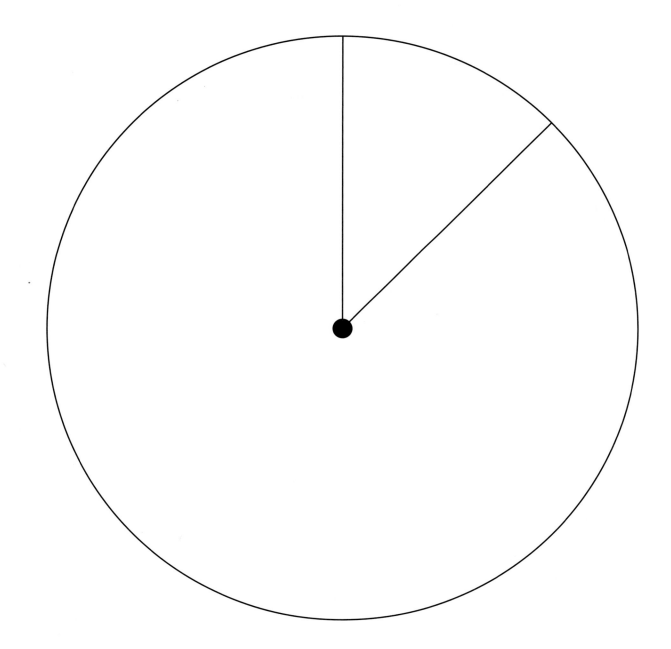 Blue

Color the smaller part of the spinner red. Red

Explore Probability **453**

Name _____

Class Activity

Vocabulary

prediction
more likely

▶ **Probability Experiment**

1. Make a **prediction**. Is it **more likely** that you will roll a total of 2 or a total of 7? _____

2. Do the experiment.

   • Toss the number cubes 30 times.

   • Use tally marks to record the totals you roll.

   • Find the number of times you got each total.

Remember

| means 1

卌 means 5

Possible Totals	**Tally Marks**	**Number**
2		
3		
4		
5		
6		
7		
8		
9		
10		
11		
12		

Explore Probability

Class Activity

▶ **Find All Possible Combinations**

Make an **organized list** to solve the problems.

---

1. Nadia has a red coat and a blue coat. She also has a yellow hat and a green hat. How many different combinations of a coat and a hat can she wear?

   ☐ different **combinations**

Coat Color		Hat Color
red	→	
red	→	
blue	→	
blue	→	

---

2. Tia has white, wheat, and rye bread. She also has ham and tuna. How many different kinds of sandwiches can she make?

   ☐ different sandwiches

Bread		Filling
white	→	
white	→	
rye	→	

---

3. Michael has blue pants and black pants. He also has a red shirt and a green shirt. How many different combinations of pants and shirts can he wear?

   ☐ different combinations

Pants Color		Shirt Color
blue	→	
blue	→	

---

4. **On the Back** Kara is buying frozen yogurt. She can buy a cone or a cup. She can get vanilla, chocolate, or mint. Make a list of all the different combinations she can buy.

Name _____

Possible Outcomes

Class Activity

Name _____

► **Math and Science**

Mr. Miller experiments with plants to see how many flowers bloom. He records data and makes graphs.

This first column in this table shows the number of flowers on three different plants in Week 1.

Number of Flowers on a Plant

Plant	Week 1	Week 2	Week 3
A	2		
B	3		
C	5		

1. In Week 2: Plant A had 3 more flowers than it did in Week 1.
Plant B had 1 more flower than it did in Week 1.
Plant C had 3 fewer flowers than it did in Week 1.

Complete the second column to show the number of flowers on each plant in Week 2.

2. In Week 3, Plant B had 1 more flower than in Week 2, and all three plants had the same number of flowers. Complete the third column to show the number of flowers on each plant in Week 3.

3. Make a bar graph to show the data in the table.

Number of Flowers on a Plant

Number of Flowers

5								
4								
3								
2								
1								

Week 1   Week 2   Week 3

KEY:

☐ plant A

☐ plant B

☐ plant C

Name _____

▶ **Supporting Math Statements**

Support each statement. Write a paragraph and make a drawing.

1. If there is an even number of objects, equal shares for two people can always be made.

_____

_____

_____

_____

2. If a shape has four sides equal in length and four square corners, the shape is a square.

_____

_____

_____

_____

Use Mathematical Processes

Name _____

1. Count by 2s. Then multiply.
Shoes

$7 \times 2 =$ ___ 14

for tean

_____

2. Count by 3s. Then multiply.
Wheels on a tricycle

$5 \times 3 =$ ___ 15

_____

3. Count by 4s. Then multiply.
Legs on a dog

$6 \times 4 =$ ___ 16

_____

4. Count by 5s. Then multiply.
Fingers on a hand

       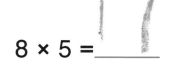

$8 \times 5 =$ ___ 17

_____

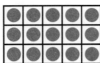

Write the numbers.

5.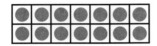

_____ × _____ or

_____ × _____

6.

_____ × _____

7.

_____ × _____ or

_____ × _____

8.

_____ × _____ or

_____ × _____

Draw in your answers. Write the numbers, too.

9. Walt has **twice** as many crayons as Carla.

Carla has _____.

Walt has _____.

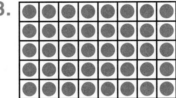

| Carla | Walt |

10. Tony has **half** as many toy cars as Harvey.

Tony has _____.

Harvey has _____.

| Tony | Harvey |

Name _____

Draw in your answers. Write the numbers, too.

11. Maria and Rachel have **equal shares** of toys.

    Maria has _____.

    Rachel has _____.

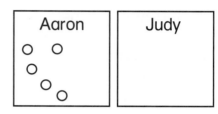

12. Judy has **double** the number of pens that Aaron has.

    Judy has _____.

    Aaron has _____.

 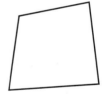

Is the figure symmetrical? Write *yes* or *no*.
If yes, draw one line of symmetry.

13.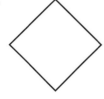

14.

15.

16.

_____   _____   _____   _____

Write the fraction for the shaded part.

17.

18.

19.

20.

_____   _____   _____   _____

Look at the bag of cubes. Circle the correct event.

21. Which event is certain?

I will pick a black cube.

I will pick a white cube.

22. Which event is impossible?

I will pick a black cube.

I will pick a white cube.

Look at the bag of cubes. How likely are you to pick a
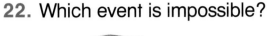 than a ⬜?

23.

more likely

less likely

24.

more likely

less likely

25. Extended Response Draw a shape and shade $\frac{3}{4}$ of it.

► **Non-Standard Units of Length**

1. Find each object. Estimate and then measure the
   length of each in small and large paper clips.

Object	Estimated length	Measured length
	about _____ ⌁ about _____ ⌁	about _____ ⌁ about _____ ⌁
	about _____ ⌁ about _____ ⌁	about _____ ⌁ about _____ ⌁

2. Are the measurement numbers larger with small or
   large paper clips? Explain.

   _____

   _____

3. Sona measured the length of a notebook using small
   paper clips. The length was 35 small paper clips. She
   then measured the same length using large paper
   clips. Was her new measurement more than 35 large
   paper clips? Explain.

   _____

   _____

Class Activity

Vocabulary
mass
capacity

▶ **Non-Standard Units of Mass**

4. List objects you might use as non-standard units of **mass**.

_____

_____

_____

_____

_____

_____

▶ **Non-Standard Units of Capacity**

5. List objects you might use as non-standard units of **capacity**.

_____

_____

_____

_____

_____

_____

Explore Measurement Concepts

Dear Family,

Your child is beginning another unit on measurement.

Children will first investigate measuring using non-standard units. They will measure length in units such as paper clips and mass in units such as pennies, using a handmade balance scale. Children will arrange containers in order of increasing capacity and test the order by transferring water from one container to another. They will also discuss ideas for measuring volume and time using non-standard units.

Children will continue to measure length in customary units. They will make their own inch ruler and yardstick to measure in inches, feet, and yards. They will also make conversions between customary units using these relationships:

1 foot = 12 inches
1 yard = 3 feet
1 yard = 36 inches

These are examples of the types of conversion they will do for homework in Lesson 2.

1 ft = _____12_____ in.   3 ft = _____36_____ in.   2 yd = _____6_____ ft

In the last lesson of this unit, children will have an opportunity to measure length, mass, weight, capacity, time, and temperature using standard units.

To help bridge your child's classroom learning with home, ask your child to estimate and measure objects that he or she uses in everyday activities. For example, you might ask, "How much do you think this pot holds?" and have your child measure its capacity in cups.

If you have any questions or comments, please call or write to me.

Sincerely,
Your child's teacher

Estimada familia:

Su niño empieza otra unidad sobre las medidas.

Los niños empezarán a medir con unidades no usuales. Medirán la longitud usando sujetapapeles y la masa usando unidades tales como monedas de un centavo con una balanza que ellos harán. Los niños ordenarán recipientes según su capacidad y comprobarán el orden pasando agua de un recipiente a otro. También comentarán ideas para medir el volumen y el tiempo usando unidades no usuales.

Más adelante, los niños medirán la longitud en unidades del sistema usual. Harán su propia regla de pulgadas y su propia regla de 1 yarda para medir en pulgadas, pies y yardas. También harán conversiones entre estas unidades utilizando las siguientes relaciones:

1 pie = 12 pulgadas
1 yarda = 3 pies
1 yarda = 36 pulgadas

Estos son ejemplos de los tipos de conversiones que harán como tarea para la Lección 2.

1 pie = _____12_____ pulg   3 pies = _____36_____ pulg

2 yd = _____6_____ pies

En la última lección de esta unidad los niños tendrán la oportunidad de medir la longitud, la masa, el peso, la capacidad, el tiempo y la temperatura usando unidades usuales de medida.

Para ayudar a su niño a hacer la conexión entre el aprendizaje en la escuela y la casa, pídale que estime y mida objetos que se usan en las actividades diarias. Por ejemplo, podría preguntarle, "¿Cuánto crees que cabe en esta olla?" y pedirle que mida su capacidad usando una taza.

Si tiene alguna duda o comentario, por favor comuníquese conmigo.

Atentamente,
El maestro de su niño

Explore Measurement Concepts

14-2

Class Activity

▶ **Make an Inch Ruler**

Directions:

Step 1: Cut along the dashed lines.

Step 2: Place the sections in the correct order.

Step 3: Tape or glue together the sections at the tab.

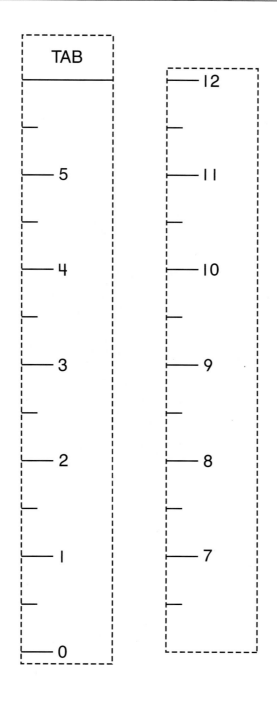

Inch Ruler

Class Activity

Name _____

Vocabulary

inch (in.)

► **Measure to the Nearest Inch**

To measure to the nearest **inch (in.)**, place the zero mark on your ruler at the left end of the object. Find the inch mark that is closest to the right end of the object.

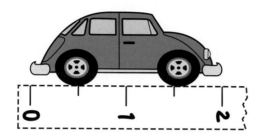

To the nearest inch, the length of this toy car is 2 inches.

Measure the length of each object to the nearest inch.

1.

_____

2.

_____

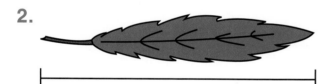

3.

_____

4. Draw a horizontal line that is 2 in. long.

5. Draw a horizontal line that is 6 in. long.

Name _____

▶ **Estimate and Measure in Inches**

6. Describe a part of your hand that measures about 2 in.

   _____

7. Describe a part of your hand that measures about 1 in.

   _____

8. Describe a part of your hand that measures about 6 in.

   _____

Estimate and measure the length of each line segment.

9. ────────────────────

   Estimated length: _____

   Measured length: _____

10. ──────────────────────────────

   Estimated length: _____

   Measured length: _____

11. Find four classroom objects that you can measure in inches. Estimate and then measure the length of each object to the nearest inch. Complete the table.

Object	Estimated length (in.)	Measured length (in.)

14-2

Class Activity

► **Make a Yardstick**

Directions:

Step 1: Cut along the dashed lines.

Step 2: Place the sections in the correct order.

Step 3: Tape or glue together the sections at the tab.

TAB	TAB	TAB	TAB	TAB	
					36
5	11	17	23	29	35
4	10	16	22	28	34
3	9	15	21	27	33
2	8	14	20	26	32
1	7	13	19	25	31
0					

Yardstick

Class Activity

Name _____

Vocabulary
foot (ft)
yard (yd)

► Measure in Feet and Yards

Find each length to the nearest **foot (ft).**

12. width of your desk

_____

13. length from your knee to your ankle

_____

Find each length to the nearest **yard (yd).**

14. height of the classroom door

_____

15. length of a bookshelf

_____

Measure each length to the nearest foot and to the nearest yard.

16. width of the classroom door

_____ ft

_____ yd

17. length of the classroom board

_____ ft

_____ yd

18. What do you notice about the numbers when you measure in yards instead of feet?

_____

► Select a Unit

Tell the unit you would use to measure the length of each object. Write _inch, foot,_ or _yard._

19.

_____

20.

_____

21.

_____

22.

_____

Class Activity

▶ Change Units

Customary Units of Length
1 ft = 12 in.
1 yd = 3 ft
1 yd = 36 in.

Complete each table.

23.

Feet	1	2	3	4	5	6
Inches	12	24				

24.

Yards	1	2	3	4	5	6
Feet	3	6				

25.

Yards	1	2	3	4	5	6
Inches	36	72				

26. Fill in the correct number.

2 ft = _____ in.   1 yd = _____ ft   24 in. = _____ ft

4 yd = _____ ft   36 in. = _____ ft   5 ft = _____ in.

Customary Units of Length

Class Activity

Vocabulary
cup
pint
quart
gallon

Use **cup**, **pint**, **quart**, and **gallon** containers to answer each question.

1. How many cups fit in a pint? _____

2. How many cups fit in a quart? _____

3. How many cups fit in a gallon? _____

4. How many pints fit in a quart? _____

5. How many pints fit in a gallon? _____

6. How many quarts fit in a gallon? _____

Find how many of each fill containers A and B.

7.

Container	Number of Cups	Number of Pints	Number of Quarts
A			
B			

Vocabulary
ounce
pound

Find classroom objects that weigh about an **ounce.**
Weigh them. Fill in the chart.

1.

Less than 1 Ounce	About 1 Ounce	More than 1 Ounce

Find classroom objects that weigh about a **pound.**
Weigh them. Fill in the chart.

2.

Less than 1 Pound	About 1 Pound	More than 1 Pound

Measurement

Measure the length of each object to the nearest inch.

1. 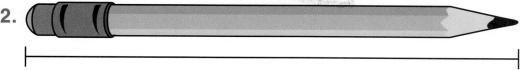 _____

2.  _____

3. _____

Fill in the correct number.

4. 1 yd = _____ in.

5. 1 ft = _____ in.

6. 1 yd = _____ ft

7. 24 in. = _____ ft

8. 9 ft = _____ yd

9. 72 in. = _____ yd

10. **Extended Response** If you measured the length of the classroom board in inches and in yards, which measure would have a larger number? Explain.

_____

_____

_____

_____

_____

_____

Use the 120 Poster.

Skip count forward and backward.

1. Start at 3. Skip count forward by 5s.
   Color each box green.

2. Start at 100. Skip count backward by 5s.
   Color each box blue.

3. Start at 119. Skip count backward by 5s.
   Color each box brown.

4. What pattern do you see for skip-counting by 5s?

   _____

   _____

5. Start at 8. Skip count forward by 10s.
   Color each box yellow.

6. Start at 100. Skip count backward by 10s.
   Circle each box.

7. Start at 92. Skip count backward by 10s.
   Color each box orange.

8. Start at 6. Skip count forward by 10s.
   Color each box red.

9. What pattern do you see for skip-counting by 10s?

   _____

   _____

Name _____

Use a calculator to skip count.
Write each number after you enter the equal sign.

1. Start at 4. Skip count forward by 10s.

   Enter (4) then (+) (1) (0) (=). Then continue entering (=).

   4, _____, _____, _____, _____, _____, _____, _____, _____, _____

2. Start at 29. Skip count forward by 10s.

   29, _____, _____, _____, _____, _____, _____, _____, _____, _____

3. Start at 91. Skip count backward by 10s.

   91, _____, _____, _____, _____, _____, _____, _____, _____, _____

4. Start at 127. Skip count backward by 10s.

   127, _____, _____, _____, _____, _____, _____, _____, _____, _____

5. Start at 4. Skip count forward by 5s.

   4, _____, _____, _____, _____, _____, _____, _____, _____, _____

6. Start at 27. Skip count forward by 5s.

   27, _____, _____, _____, _____, _____, _____, _____, _____, _____

7. Start at 86. Skip count backward by 5s.

   86, _____, _____, _____, _____, _____, _____, _____, _____, _____

8. Start at 63. Skip count backward by 5s.

   63, _____, _____, _____, _____, _____, _____, _____, _____, _____

Count Different Ways

Class Activity

Name _____

Use the **line graph** to answer the questions.

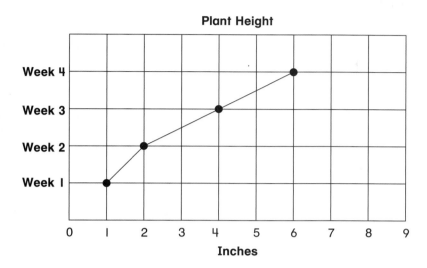

Plant Height

1. What is the title of the graph? _____

2. How much time does this graph represent?

   _____

3. What change is happening over the weeks?

   _____

4. How much did the plant grow between
   Week 1 and Week 2? _____

5. How much did the plant grow between
   Week 2 and Week 3? _____

6. How much did the plant grow between
   Week 3 and Week 4? _____

7. How much did the plant grow between
   Week 1 and Week 4? _____

Class Activity

Name _____

Use the line graph to answer the questions.

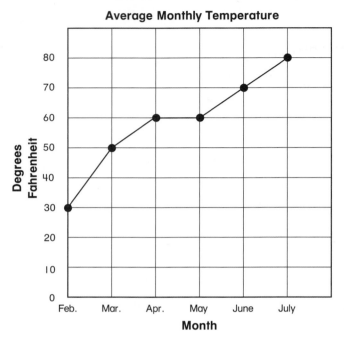

1. What is the title of the graph? _____

2. How much time does this graph represent?

   _____

3. What change is happening over the months?

   _____

4. How much did the temperature rise between February and March? _____

5. How much did the temperature rise between March and April? _____

6. How much did the temperature rise between May and June? _____

7. Between which two months did the temperature stay the same? _____

8. Between which two months did the temperature rise the most? _____

Change Over Time

Name _____

Class Activity

Use the **three-dimensional shapes** to predict and build new shapes.

1. Predict what shape you can make by combining a cube and a pyramid. Then combine the 2 shapes and draw the shape they make.

2. Predict what shape you can make by combining a rectangular prism and a cylinder. Then combine the 2 shapes and draw the shape they make.

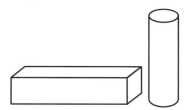

3. Predict what shape you can make by combining a cylinder, a rectangular prism, and a pyramid. Then combine the 3 shapes and draw the shape they make.

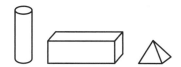

Name _____

Class Activity

Use clay to make the named shape.
Then predict and cut apart the shape to make new shapes.

1. Predict what shapes you will make by cutting apart a cube.
   Then cut the shape and draw the new shapes.

2. Predict what shapes you will make by cutting apart a sphere.
   Then cut the shape and draw the new shapes.

3. Predict what shapes you will make by cutting apart a pyramid.
   Then cut the shape and draw the new shapes.

Explore 3-Dimensional Shapes

Glossary

add

•••• ••
4 + 2 = 6

addend

5 + 6 = 11
↑   ↑
addends

Adding Up Method (for Subtraction)

144
− 68
76

68 + 2 = 70
70 + 30 = 100
100 + 44 = 144

76

after

98, 99

99 is after 98.

A.M.

The hours between midnight and noon.

angle

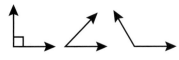

These are angles.

area

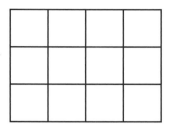

Area = 12 square units

You can find the area of a figure by covering it with square units and counting them.

array

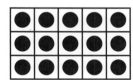

This picture shows a 3 × 5 or 5 × 3 array.

bar graph

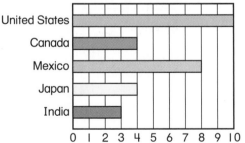

Coins in My Collection

horizontal bar graph

Flowers in My Garden

vertical bar graph

Glossary (Continued)

before

3 1, 32

31 is before 32.

between

8 1, 82, 83

82 is between 8 1 and 83.

break-apart

You can break apart a larger number to get two smaller amounts called break-aparts.

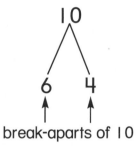

break-aparts of 1 0

C

calendar

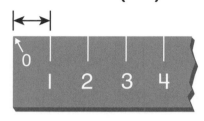

capacity

Capacity is how much a container holds. This container holds 1 quart of milk.

cent

front   back

1 cent or 1¢ or $0.01

centimeter (cm)

certain

You are certain to choose a black button from the jar.

change minus problem

Sarah had 1 2 books.
Then she loaned her friend 9 books.
How many books does Sarah have now?

$$12 - 9 = \boxed{3}$$

had   loaned   now

Any number may be unknown.

change plus problem

Alvin had 9 toy cars.
Then he got 3 more.
How many toy cars does he have now?

9 + 3 = $\boxed{12}$

had   got   now

Any number may be unknown.

collection problem

Jason put 8 large plates and 4 small plates on the table. How many plates are on the table altogether?

8 + 4 = $\boxed{12}$

large   small   altogether

Any number may be unknown.

circle graph

Animals at Grasslands Nature Park

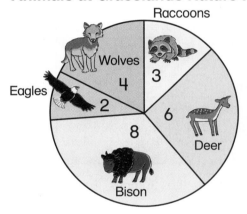

comparison problem

Joe has 6 roses. Sasha has 9 roses.
How many more roses does Sasha have than Joe?

J   S

6 + $\boxed{}$ = 9

9 − 6 = $\boxed{3}$

S   J

cone

clock

analog clock

digital clock

congruent

These are congruent figures.   These are not congruent figures.

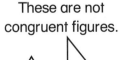

Congruent figures have the same size and shape.

Glossary (Continued)

count all

$5 + 3 = \square$

1 2 3 4 5   6 7 8

• • • • •   • • •

$5 + 3 = \boxed{8}$

count by/count-bys

I can count by 2s.

2, 4, 6, 8, 10, 12, 14, 16, 18, and 20 are 2s count-bys.

count on

$5 + 3 = \boxed{8}$

$5 + \boxed{3} = 8$

$8 - 5 = \boxed{3}$

Already **5**

cube

cylinder

D

data

	Hamsters	Mice
Kendra	5	8
Scott	2	9
Ida	7	3

data

The data in the table show how many hamsters and how many mice each child has.

day

November						
Sun	Mon	Tues	Wed	Thurs	Fri	Sat
	1	2	3	4	5	6
7	8	9	10	11	12	13
14	15	16	17	18	19	20
21	22	23	24	25	26	27
28	39	30				

November has 30 days. Each day has 24 hours.

decade numbers

10, 20, 30, 40, 50, 60, 70, 80, 90

decade partners

20 and 80 are decade partners of 100.

decimal point

$4.25

decimal point

Expanded Method (for Subtraction)

$$64 = \overset{50}{\cancel{60}} + \overset{14}{\cancel{4}}$$
$$- 28 = 20 + 8$$
$$\overline{30 + 6 = 36}$$

expanded number

$283 = 200 + 80 + 3$

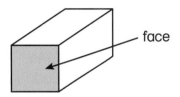
F

face

face

fair shares

fewer

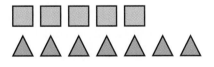

There are fewer ▢ than △.

flip

You can **flip** a figure over a **horizontal line**.

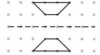

You can **flip** a figure over a **vertical line**.

foot (ft)

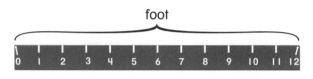

foot

12 inches = 1 foot
(not drawn to scale)

fourth

 1 whole

 $\frac{1}{4}$

$\frac{1}{4}$ (one fourth) of the square is shaded.

fraction

4 equal parts

$\frac{3}{4}$ is 3 out of 4 equal parts.

$\frac{3}{4} = \frac{1}{4} + \frac{1}{4} + \frac{1}{4}$

Glossary (Continued)

front-end estimation

$$\begin{array}{r} \text{③}4 \longrightarrow 30 \\ +\text{①}5 \longrightarrow +10 \\ \hline 40 \end{array}$$

function table

Add 3.	
0	3
1	4
2	5
3	6

G

greater than

° ° ° °   ° ° ° ° °

34   >   25

34 is greater than 25.

greatest

25   41   63

63 is the greatest number.

group name

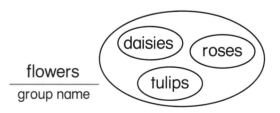

flowers
group name

growing pattern

A number or geometric pattern that increases.

Examples: 2, 4, 6, 8, 10...

1, 2, 5, 10, 17...

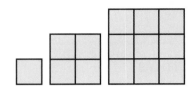

H

half

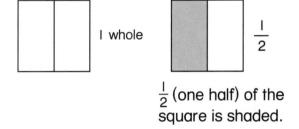

1 whole

$\frac{1}{2}$

$\frac{1}{2}$ (one half) of the square is shaded.

half-hour

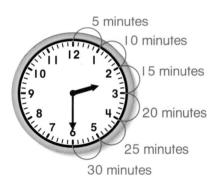

5 minutes
10 minutes
15 minutes
20 minutes
25 minutes
30 minutes

30 minutes = 1 half-hour

hidden information

Heather bought a dozen eggs. She used 7 of them to make breakfast. How many eggs does she have left?

$12 - 7 = \boxed{5}$

The hidden information is that a dozen means 12.

horizontal

$$4 + 5 = 9$$

horizontal form

horizontal line

hour

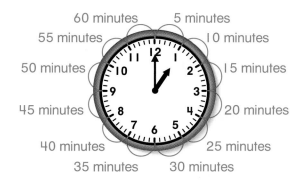

60 minutes   5 minutes
55 minutes   10 minutes
50 minutes   15 minutes
45 minutes   20 minutes
40 minutes   25 minutes
35 minutes   30 minutes

60 minutes = 1 hour

hour hand

hour hand

hundreds

3 hundreds

347 has 3 hundreds.

↑

hundreds

I

impossible

It is impossible to choose a white button from this jar.

inch (in.)

1 inch

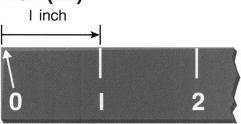

0   1   2

K

key

Apples Bought

Red	🍎 🍎 🍎 🍎
Green	🍎 🍎
Yellow	🍎 🍎

Key: Each 🍎 stands for 2 apples.

L

least

14   7   63

7 is the least number.

length

The length of the pencil is about 17 cm.

Glossary (Continued)

less likely

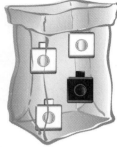

It is less likely that I will choose a black cube than a white cube if I choose a cube without looking.

less than

$$45 \quad < \quad 46$$

45 is less than 46.

line

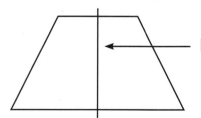

line of symmetry

line of symmetry

line segment

Make a Ten

$$8 + 6 = \boxed{}$$

$8 \bullet\bullet | \bullet\bullet\bullet\bullet$

$10 + 4$

$10 + 4 = 14,$

so $8 + 6 = 14$

make change

Sellers make change when they give back money when a buyer pays too much.

mass

You can use a balance scale to compare mass.

matching drawing

fewer

more

Math Mountain

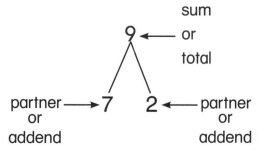

sum
or
total

9

partner
or
addend

7   2

partner
or
addend

S10 Glossary

measure

You measure to find the length, weight, mass, capacity, volume, or temperature of an object. You find how many units.

meter(m)

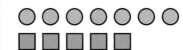

100 centimeters = 1 meter
(not drawn to scale)

midpoint

midpoint

The point exactly halfway between the ends of a line segment is the midpoint.

minus

8 − 3 = 5

8 minus 3 equals 5.

$$\begin{array}{r} 8 \\ -\ 3 \\ \hline 5 \end{array}$$

minute

I minute

60 seconds = 1 minute

minute hand

minute hand: points to the minutes

money string

$1.00 = 25¢ + 25¢ + 25¢ + 10¢ + 10¢ + 5¢

month

June						
Sun	Mon	Tues	Wed	Thurs	Fri	Sat
				1	2	3
4	5	6	7	8	9	10
11	12	13	14	15	16	17
18	19	20	21	22	23	24
25	26	27	28	29	30	

June is the sixth month. There are twelve months in a year.

more

There are more ◯ than ▧.

more likely

It is more likely that I will choose a black button than a white button if I choose a button without looking.

Glossary (Continued)

multiply

$3 \times 5 = 15$

$5 + 5 + 5$

3 fives

not equal to

$6 + 4 \neq 8$

$6 + 4$ is not equal to 8.

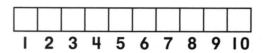

N

New Groups Above Method

$\overset{1}{56}$
$+ 28$
$\overline{84}$

$6 + 8 = 14$

The 1 new ten in 14 goes up to the tens place.

number line

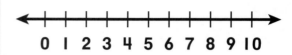

0 1 2 3 4 5 6 7 8 9 10

This is a number line.

New Groups Below Method

56
$+ 2\underset{1}{8}$
$\overline{84}$

$6 + 8 = 14$

The 1 new ten in 14 goes below in the tens place.

number path

1	2	3	4	5	6	7	8	9	10

This is a number path.

nickel

front   back

5 cents or 5¢ or $0.05

numerator

$\frac{3}{4}$ ← numerator

$\frac{3}{4} = \frac{1}{4} + \frac{1}{4} + \frac{1}{4}$

The numerator tells how many unit fractions.

non-standard unit

The length of the pencil is 5 paper clips.

A paper clip is a non-standard unit of length. An inch and a centimeter are standard units of length.

O

odd number

A number is odd if you can make groups of 2 and have one left over.

9 is an odd number.

ones

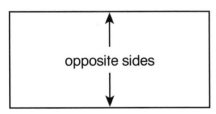

7 ones

347 has 7 ones.

↑
ones

opposite sides

opposite sides

order

2, 5, 6

The numbers 2, 5, and 6 are in order from least to greatest.

ordinal number

Ordinal numbers name positions.

| 1st | 2nd | 3rd | 4th |
| first | second | third | fourth |

P

parallel

Lines or line segments that are always the same distance apart.

parallelogram

A parallelogram has 2 pairs of parallel sides.

Partner House

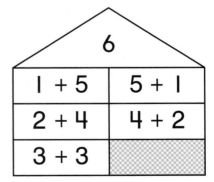

Glossary (Continued)

partner lengths

partner lengths of 4 cm

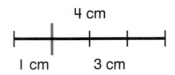

4 cm

1 cm   3 cm

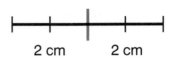

2 cm   2 cm

partners

9 + 6 = 15

↑   ↑

partners

addends

pattern

2, 4, 6, 8, 10, 12

These are patterns.

penny

front   back

1 cent or 1¢ or $0.01

perimeter

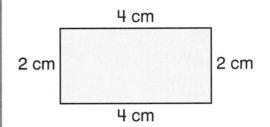

4 cm

2 cm   2 cm

4 cm

perimeter = 2 cm + 4 cm + 2 cm + 4 cm = 12 cm

Perimeter is the total length of the sides.

pictograph

Apples Bought

Red	🍎 🍎 🍎 🍎
Green	🍎 🍎
Yellow	🍎 🍎

Key: Each 🍎 stands for 2 apples.

picture graph

| Flowers | 🌸 🌸 🌸 🌸 🌸 |
| Vases | 🏺 🏺 🏺 🏺 🏺 🏺 🏺 |

pie graph

Animals at Grasslands Nature Park

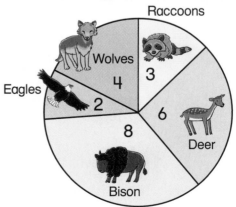

Raccoons

Wolves 4

3

Eagles 2

8

6 Deer

Bison

same as a circle graph

plus

$3 + 2 = 5$

3 plus 2 equals 5.
$$\begin{array}{r} 3 \\ + 2 \\ \hline 5 \end{array}$$

P.M.

The hours between noon and midnight.

polygons

Polygons have sides that are line segments.

possible

It is possible to choose a white button.
It is possible to choose a black button.

predict

I think it will rain tomorrow.

I predict that it will rain tomorrow.

probability

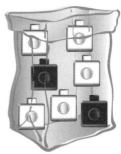

· What is the probability of choosing a white cube?
· It is likely.

proof drawing

Proof Drawing

$86 + 57 = 143$

pyramids

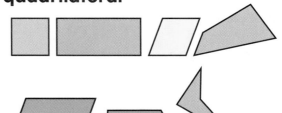

Q

quadrilateral

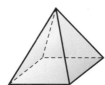

A quadrilateral has 4 sides.

Glossary (Continued)

quarter

front   back

25 cents or 25¢ or $0.25

Quick Hundreds

347

Quick Hundreds

Quick Tens

162

Quick Tens

R

rectangle

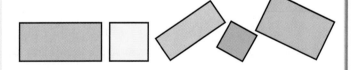

A rectangle has 4 sides and
4 right angles.

rectangular prism

regular polygons

A regular polygon has all sides and all
angles equal.

repeating pattern

A pattern consisting of a group of numbers,
letters, or figures that repeat.

Examples: 1, 2, 1, 2, …

A, B, C, A, B, C, …

right angle

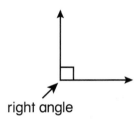

right angle

rotation

You can **turn** or **rotate** a figure around a point.

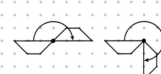

round

44 is closer to 40 than 50.

44 rounds to 40.

Show All Totals Method

$$\begin{array}{r} 25 \\ +\ 48 \\ \hline 60 \\ 13 \\ \hline 73 \end{array} \qquad \begin{array}{r} 724 \\ +\ 158 \\ \hline 12 \\ 70 \\ 800 \\ \hline 882 \end{array}$$

ruler

A ruler is used to measure length.

S

scale

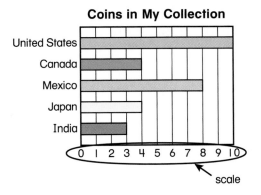

The numbers along the side or the bottom of a graph.

similar

These figures are similar. These figures are similar. These figures are not similar.

Similar figures always have the same shape and sometimes have the same size.

situation equation

A baker baked 100 loaves of bread. He sold some loaves. There are 73 loaves left. How many loaves of bread did he sell?

situation equation

skip count

skip count by 2s: 2, 4, 6, 8, . . .
skip count by 5s: 5, 10, 15, 20, . . .

sequence

Sequences follow a pattern.

2, 4, 6, . . .

9, 8, 7, . . .

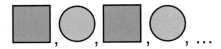

Glossary (Continued)

slide

You can **slide** a figure right or left along a straight line.

You can slide a figure up or down along a straight line.

solution equation

A baker baked 100 loaves of bread. He sold some loaves. There are 73 loaves left. How many loaves of bread did he sell?

$$100 - 73 = \boxed{}$$

solution equation

sphere

square

A square has 4 equal sides and 4 right angles.

square centimeter

Each side measures 1 centimeter.

1 square centimeter

square unit

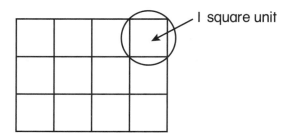

I square unit

The area of this rectangle is 12 square units.

standard unit

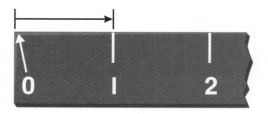

An inch is a standard unit of length.
A paper clip is a non-standard unit of length.

subtract

$$8 - 5 = 3$$

sum

$$4 + 3 = 7$$

sum

$$\begin{array}{r} 4 \\ + 3 \\ \hline 7 \end{array}$$

sum

survey

To collect data by asking people questions.

switch the partners

Show partners in a different order.

$$6 + 4 = 10 \qquad 4 + 6 = 10$$

partners   partners

The total is the same.

symmetry

A figure has symmetry if it can be folded along a line so that the two halves match exactly.

teen number

any number from 11 to 19

11 12 13 14 15 16 17 18 19

temperature

A thermometer measures the temperature.

T

---

table

	Hamsters	Mice
Kendra	5	8
Scott	2	9
Ida	7	3

tally chart

Favorite Color	Tally Marks	Number of Students
red	||||	4
blue	|||||		6
yellow	||||| ||	7

tens

4 tens

347 has 4 tens.

tens

third

1 whole

$\frac{1}{3}$

$\frac{1}{3}$ (one third) of the square is shaded.

Glossary (Continued)

thousand

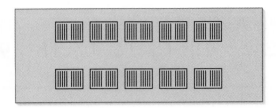

1,000 = ten hundreds

time

	January					
Sun	Mon	Tues	Wed	Thurs	Fri	Sat
1	2	3	4	5	6	7
8	9	10	11	12	13	14
15	16	17	18	19	20	21
22	23	24	25	26	27	28
29	30	31				

Time is measured in hours, minutes, seconds, days, weeks, months, and years.

total

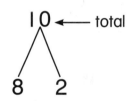

10 ← total

8   2

triangle

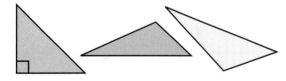

A triangle has 3 sides.

turn

You can **turn** or **rotate** a figure around a point.

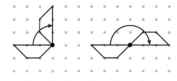

twice

Jeremy

Michael

Jeremy has twice as many books as Michael.

U

ungroup

$$\begin{array}{r} 12 \\ 0\ 2\ 14 \\ \cancel{1\ 3\ 4} \\ -\ \ 7\ 8 \\ \hline 5\ 6 \end{array}$$

Ungroup when you need more ones or tens to subtract.

Ungroup First Method

$$\begin{array}{r} 6\ 4 \\ -\ 2\ 8 \\ \uparrow\ \uparrow \end{array}$$
yes no

1. Check to see if there are enough tens and ones to subtract.

$$\begin{array}{r} 5\ 14 \\ \cancel{6}\ \cancel{4} \\ -\ 2\ 8 \end{array}$$

2. You can get more ones by taking from the tens and putting them in the ones place.

$$\begin{array}{r} 5\ 14 \\ \cancel{6}\ \cancel{4} \\ -\ 2\ 8 \\ \hline 3\ 6 \end{array}$$

3. Subtract from either right to left or left to right.

unknown

$3 + \boxed{} = 9$

unknown partner

$3 + 6 = \boxed{}$

unknown total

V

Venn diagram

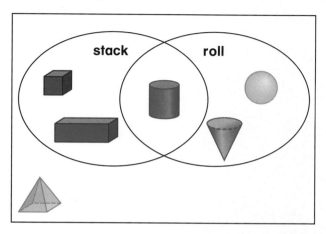

vertex

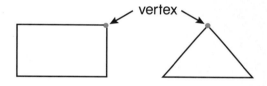

vertical

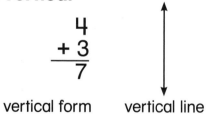

vertical form   vertical line

view

This is the side view of the rectangular prism above.

volume

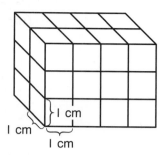

The volume of this rectangular prism is 24 cubic centimeters.

W

weight

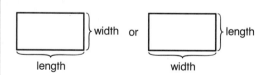

The weight of this book is 2 pounds.

width

Glossary (Continued)

word name

12

twelve ← word name

Y

yard (yd)

3 feet = 1 yard (not drawn to scale)